THE ROVER

THE ROVER

or

The Banished Cavaliers

Aphra Behn

edited by Anne Russell

a broadview literary text

Canadian Cataloguing in Publication Data

Behn, Aphra, 1640-1689
    The rover
(Broadview literary texts)

ISBN 1-55111-037-7

I. Russell, Anne Elizabeth, 1952-   . II. Title.
III. Series.

PR3317.R58 1994 822'.4 C94-9930552-9

Broadview Press
Post Office Box 1243, Peterborough, Ontario, Canada K9J 7H5

in the United States of America:
3576 California Road, Orchard Park, NY 14127

in the United Kingdom:
B.R.A.D. Book Representation & Distribution Ltd.,
244A, London Road, Hadleigh, Essex. SS7 2DE

Broadview Press gratefully acknowledges the support of the Canada Council, the Ontario Arts Council, and the Ministry of Canadian Heritage.

PRINTED IN CANADA

Contents

Acknowledgments

It is a pleasure to acknowledge the assistance of the many people and organizations I have been helped by in the preparation of this edition.

Wilfrid Laurier University contributed financial support for the work with an Initiatory Grant and later a Book Preparation Grant.

Throughout the preparation of this edition, I have relied on the knowledge and assistance of librarians and library staff in many institutions, including the Wilfrid Laurier University Library, Dana Porter Library and Doris Lewis Rare Book Room of the University of Waterloo, Robarts Library and Thomas Fisher Rare Book Library of the University of Toronto, the Metropolitan Toronto Reference Library, Bata Library of Trent University, the Library of the Covent Garden Theatre Museum, and the British Library.

Betty Blake and Tim Snider of the New Oxford English Dictionary at the University of Waterloo generously allowed me to use their computer facilities, and helped me search the New Oxford English Dictionary with the software they are developing.

Joanne Buchan and Sandra Wallace, secretaries of the Wilfrid Laurier English Department, gave advice and assistance with many technical questions, as did the staff of Computing Services at Wilfrid Laurier University. The staff of Broadview Press have been unfailingly friendly and helpful. George Kirkpatrick deserves special thanks.

I am especially grateful to the friends and colleagues who helped me immeasurably, in many ways, at different stages of the preparation of the edition, particularly Viviana Comensoli, Veronica Hollinger, Michael Neumann, Manal Stamboulie, Fred Tromly, Eleanor Ty, Lynn Shakinovsky, and Lisa Vargo.

Above all, I thank my husband Martin Ridley Dowding, whose intellectual, editorial and research support has been constant, and greatly appreciated.

Introduction

Aphra Behn's Life and Career

Aphra Behn was an extraordinary woman for her time. Her life was not confined by the boundaries normally accepted by seventeenth-century women, whose spheres of influence were the domestic and private. Instead, Behn's was an unusually independent and public life. In her youth she had lived in Surinam, now Dutch Guiana; a few years later she acted as an English agent in the Low Countries during the war between the Dutch and English in the mid-1660s. She is believed to have had a romantic relationship with a lawyer named John Hoyle, an association which has led many critics and biographers to speculate about her sexual life.[1] An outspoken Tory and strong supporter of the monarchy, Behn had some social and professional connections with members of the English court of King Charles II.

Although Behn was not the first woman to publish her writing, she was the first professional woman writer in England. She belonged to the literary and theatrical society of London, where she had a wide acquaintance and was on good terms with professional authors such as John Dryden and Thomas Otway as well as with well-known performers. For nineteen years she made her living as a playwright, translator, poet, and novelist. Her plays were a significant part of the repertory of the Restoration and early eighteenth-century theatre; *The Rover*, her most popular play, was performed in London virtually every year from 1703 to 1750.

Her works remained popular well into the mid-eighteenth century, after which her plays, including *The Rover*, virtually disappeared from the stage, partly because their frank analyses of sexual mores were seen as a sign that Behn herself was an indelicate, immoral woman.[2]

Recently there has been a resurgence of interest in Behn's writing, but since the early years of the twentieth century there has been an even greater fascination with her life. Detailed biographical studies have been published by Vita Sackville-West (1928), Walter and Clare Jerrold (1929), George Woodcock (1948), W.J. Cameron (1961), Maureen Duffy (1971), Angeline Goreau (1980), and Sara Heller Mendelson (1987). Behn's life has been treated fictionally in Beth Herst's 1992 play, *A Woman's Comedy*.[3]

Behn's biographers share a common difficulty in their efforts to understand the process by which she became a professional writer. Virtually no documented information about her early life and family circumstances is known to exist. Estimates of her year of birth range from 1640 to as late as 1649. Different late seventeenth-century sources give her birthplace as Canterbury, Sturry, or Wye, all in the county of Kent in southeast England. Her birth name has been given as Johnson or Amis, but searches of baptismal records in Canterbury, Sturry, Wye, and district, where the name Aphra was known in the 1640s, have turned up no entry which unequivocally refers to Behn.[4] When she was earning a living in London's theatrical world her name often appeared in financial and literary documents; nevertheless many elements of Behn's life and career are unknown. Consequently, most studies of Behn's life are characterized by conjecture at many points, a problem which Angeline Goreau acknowledges in the title of her biography, *Reconstructing Aphra: A Social Biography*. Because of the paucity of documents, many commentators are forced to rely on seventeenth-century anecdotes, literary references, and anonymous biographical accounts. To supplement these meager resources, Behn's biographers have used her poetic, dramatic, and fictional works to construct a more detailed, but necessarily speculative, account of her private life. The conflation of Behn's works and life is not a new phenomenon; her love poetry in particular has been read as at least partly autobiographical by many critics since the seventeenth century.[5] I am indebted to Behn's many biographers for the information in the brief account of her life which follows.[6]

The first biographical study of Behn's life is the anonymous "Memoirs of the Life of Mrs. Behn. Written by a Gentlewoman of her Acquaintance." This narrative does not have a great deal of documentary authority, but as the first extant seventeenth-century published account, it has served as the starting point for virtually all subsequent discussions of Behn's personal life. It was published after Behn's death as an introduction to her *Histories and Novels* (London, 1696); a longer version, "The History of the Life and Memoirs of Mrs. Behn" precedes the "Third Edition" of 1698.[7] Although the author of the "Life and Memoirs" signs it "one of the Fair Sex," some critics argue that it might have been written by Charles Gildon, the first editor of Behn's prose works.

According to the memoir, Behn's father, named Johnson, was a gentleman in Canterbury who was appointed Lieutenant General of Surinam by his relative Lord Willoughby. However, the father died on the voyage and, after a short stay, she returned to England, where she married Mr. Behn, a "merchant... of Dutch extraction." A note in the margin of another seventeenth-century document, a manuscript poem by Anne Finch, Duchess of Winchelsea, states that "Mrs. Behn was daughter to a barber, who lived formerly in Wye" (quoted Goreau 9). Another early record, a memoir by Thomas Culpepper, states that Behn was born at Canterbury or Sturry, and that her mother was Culpepper's nurse.[8] However, no uncontroverted documentary evidence has been located regarding Behn's place of birth or family connections.

Another frequently used source for Behn's early life is her prose fiction *Oroonoko* (1688), set in Surinam and narrated in the first person. The female narrator relates that with her mother and brother she accompanies her father to Surinam where he is to be Lieutenant General, but he dies on the voyage. In the colony, she stays in the best house, where she meets a slave whose unsuccessful revolt is the subject of the plot. Since the narrator's account agrees so closely with statements made in the "Memoirs," there has been some debate as to whether *Oroonoko* might have been the source for its details about Behn's Surinam experience.

There is other evidence that Behn actually did spend some time in Surinam (summarized by Goreau 44-45). H.G. Platt demonstrates that many of the narrator's descriptions of the landscape, history, and politics of the colony are accurate. Arguing that *Oroonoko* is partially autobiographical, W.J.

Cameron distinguishes between "the autobiographical comments which are not an integral part of the story of the Negro prince" and those "that are part of the central plot" (Cameron 6) — a fine distinction which he does not discuss in detail. Cameron relies on letters from the colony and other documents to argue that "the external evidence does not destroy the authenticity of Aphra's autobiography, but in fact strengthens it" (13); he dates Behn's arrival in Surinam "towards the end of 1663" and her departure as "before the beginning of March 1663/4" (10). According to Thomas Southerne's "Dedicatory Epistle" to his play *Oroonoko* (1696), adapted from Behn's novel, a friend of hers told Southerne that Behn "always told [Oroonoko's] story more feelingly than she writ it" (Southerne 4). Critical debate continues about how many details of *Oroonoko*, and Behn's other first-person narratives, recount the "real" Behn's life, and how many describe the narrator's character.

Although many biographers state that some time after Behn's departure from Surinam she married Mr. Behn, the "merchant... of Dutch extraction" mentioned in the "History... and Memoirs," no record of this marriage exists; nor does Behn herself mention a marriage or a husband in any known source. Some critics conclude that she may never have married, while others argue that her husband might have died in the plague of 1665.[9] In any case, in 1666 Behn was signing her correspondence "AB" and "A Behn" (Cameron 42,64).

That year, Behn was in Antwerp where she was a spy for the government of Charles II. Her mission was to acquire military and political information from William Scot, who had been in Surinam at the same time as Behn and who was rumored to have been romantically associated with her there.[10] A series of letters between Behn and her contacts at Whitehall — Major Halsall, Thomas Killigrew, and Lord Arlington — evoke a frustrating relationship, in which the correspondents frequently seem to be at cross purposes (many of Behn's later letters include pleas for expense money).[11] Cameron transcribes a letter which includes information about a Dutch plot to sink ships and block the Thames (72-74), but critics disagree on whether the information would have been useful to her contacts at Whitehall at the time she sent it (Cameron 27; Hargreaves "Warning" 203-205). By 1668, Behn was back in London and in debt. Several letters survive in which she asks for money to pay bills incurred in Antwerp. It seems she was committed to debtor's prison (Cameron 33; Goreau 115), but it is not known how long she stayed or on what terms she was released.

Aphra Behn's first play, produced by the Duke's Company at Dorset Garden Theatre in 1670, was *The Forced Marriage*, a theme she would examine in many subsequent works including *The Rover*. What we know of her subsequent career is documented in the records of the production and publication of her numerous plays,[12] fictional prose narratives, translations and poems. In addition, the addresses to readers of her published plays contain some of Behn's public statements about her work and career. Contemporary references to her life and work exist in a number of sources as do some records of her financial transactions. Discussing the latter, Goreau repeatedly notes her generosity to friends even when she herself was in need (see also Mendelson 152).

How Behn became a playwright is unknown. Some commentators suggest that she might have been introduced to the theatre by Thomas Killigrew, who was patentee of one of the two theatres in London at the time as well as one of the officials of King Charles's government with whom Behn corresponded during and after her mission to Antwerp. Whatever help he might have given her, he did not accept her play for production by his own company, the King's Company (she was associated with the Duke's Company). Behn later adapted Killigrew's *Thomaso, or The Wanderer* as a source for *The Rover*. In the "Postscript" to the play, she defends herself from imputed charges of having plagiarized *Thomaso* "which made the booksellers fear some trouble from the proprietor of that admirable play," an indication that she may not have had Killigrew's permission to adapt the play. Behn's defence explicitly challenges her readers to compare her work with *Thomaso*. She writes, "As for the words and characters, I leave the reader to judge and compare 'em with *Thomaso*, to whom I recommend the great entertainment of reading it," a statement which may or may not be sarcastic.

However it was that Behn first became associated with the theatre, she developed into a skilled playwright whose plays were produced frequently during most of her professional career. Her first play, *The Forced Marriage*, was a tragicomedy, but she soon adopted the fashion for comedy, her most successful genre. By the time *The Rover* was first performed and published in 1677, Behn had seen six of her plays produced.[13] Yet, *The Rover* first appeared anonymously, with a line in the prologue referring to the author as "he" and "him."

Apparently, Behn did not at first acknowledge the play as her own. There are a number of possible explanations. As a woman playwright, she was an anomalous figure. She wrote her first seven plays (including *The Rover*) without dedications to patrons, an unusually long period for a writer to remain without patronage, and an indication of her status outside "the usual system of contacts and patronage" (Payne 107). At every stage of her career, she was attacked for indelicacy and immorality, both inappropriate for a woman writer.[14] Perhaps the most famous criticism of her is Dryden's. After Behn's death he wrote a letter of advice to Elizabeth Thomas, who had sent him some of her poems:

> you, who write only for your Diversion, may pass your Hours with Pleasure in it, and without Prejudice, always avoiding (as I know you will) the Licenses which Mrs. Behn allowed herself, of writing loosely, and giving, (if I may have leave to say so) some Scandal to the Modesty of her Sex. I confess, I am the last Man who ought, in Justice to arraign her, who have been myself too much a Libertine in most of my poems. (Ward 127)

Although Dryden acknowledges that his approach is similar to Behn's, he criticizes her work as immodest, particularly for a woman writer, and perhaps for a woman reader.

Behn frequently complains that her writing is judged by harsher standards than those applied to men. In the "Prologue" of *The Lucky Chance* (1687) she suggests that women are especially likely to criticize her. She assures women readers that the play has been read by "several Ladys of very great Quality and unquestioned Fame, and received their most favourable Opinion" (Summers 3:187). In "To the Reader" in *Sir Patient Fancy* (1678) she bitterly complains of

> the most unjust and silly aspersion, Woman could invent to cast on Woman; and which only my being a Woman has procured me; *That it was baudy*, the least and most Excusable fault in the Men writers, to whose Plays they all crowd, as if they came to no other end than to hear what they condemn in this: *but from a Woman it was unnaturall*. (Summers 4:7)

Behn also faced charges of plagiarism for using earlier plays as sources for her own, a practice which was widespread in the seventeenth-century theatre. In response to these attacks, Behn frequently points out that her themes and dramatic practices are similar to those of male writers. Perhaps her best-known statement on the topic occurs in the "Preface" to *The Lucky Chance* which tacitly acknowledges that writing is not a feminine activity, but a masculine one:

> All I ask, is the Priviledge [sic] for my Masculine Part the Poet in me... to tread in those successful Paths my Predecessors have so long thriv'd in... If I must not, because of my Sex, have this Freedom, but that you will usurp all to your selves; I lay down my Quill, and you shall hear no more of me... for I am not content to write for a Third day only.[15] I value Fame as much as if I had been born a *Hero*; and if you rob me of that, I can retire from the ungrateful World and scorn its fickle Favours. (Summers 3:187)

In suggesting that writing is the production of "my Masculine Part the Poet," Behn attempts to establish herself as an exception — an extraordinary woman who has within her a "masculine" talent for poetry and heroism, and who asks for the "Priviledge" of exercising those qualities. She offers to stop writing if she "must not, because of my Sex, have this freedom." Yet this relatively submissive statement is qualified by her identification of herself as a "*Hero*" who "can retire" if necessary. The passage shifts from a request for the privilege of expressing her "Masculine Part" to a more confident and assertive description of herself as a "*Hero.*"

Behn's representation of herself as an exception is accurate since, as far as we know, she was the only woman writing professionally at this time.[16] Her public profile as a woman writer had many implications, one of which was her association with other "public women" — especially actresses, with whom she had professional contacts and for whom she wrote dramatic roles. Like women writers, actresses were defining new places for themselves in the public and professional spheres. Behn was thus part of the first generation of English women to participate, as writers and performers, in the representation of women characters in the theatre. Yet at the same time, the places of women as characters and performers were being culturally defined.

During the first part of the seventeenth century, in the public theatre of Shakespeare and other playwrights of the Jacobean and Caroline periods, all women's roles had been played by male performers, usually boys. At court, however, in private performances, women had performed in masques, combinations of music, poetry, dancing and allegorical spectacle. Queen Henrietta Maria, King Charles I's wife, had written and performed in a court masque; Queen Anne, King James's wife, had appeared in non-speaking parts in some of Ben Jonson's masques. However, these exceptional performances by women had been frequently attacked, especially by Puritan commentators (Ferris 65-67). In 1642, after the defeat of royalist forces in the Civil War, Parliament decreed that the theatres in London should close. While some private theatrical and operatic performances were still staged, the flourishing public theatre virtually disappeared until 1660 and the restoration of the monarchy.

In 1660, two theatre companies — the King's and the Duke's — were given charters to perform, and they attempted to recover the repertory and acting traditions which had existed before 1642. At first, women's roles were again played by male actors. But soon after the theatres re-opened, an anonymous woman played Desdemona, becoming the first actress to perform on a public English stage. King Charles II decreed in 1660 that actresses should play women's roles so that plays would be "useful and instructive representations of human life" (quoted Ferris 70), possibly a response to those who claimed that boy actors of women's roles elicited the passions of male spectators. Yet if Restoration actresses were introduced as agents of morality, they were soon blamed for introducing immorality to the theatre. As late as the early twentieth century, theatre historian Allardyce Nicoll expresses the conventional belief that "the male spectators looked upon these actresses as little better than prostitutes" (1:70-71). Certainly many Restoration actresses were the mistresses of courtiers; one of the most famous, Nell Gwyn, had a child by Charles II. But when Nicoll asserts that "the actresses" as a class were responsible for "dragging down the playhouse" (71), his condemnation is overwrought.[17]

Many recent accounts of the Restoration theatre acknowledge the pressures which men in the audience exerted on the actresses, and consider the "immorality" of the theatre as an expression of the cultural context rather than the responsibility of the actresses. Women who became performers in the late seventeenth century were often orphans or alienated from their families. Since women rarely engaged in commerce outside of a family business, almost the only way an unmarried woman could earn a living was as a servant. Acting must have seemed an attractive alternative to service. Once employed, most actresses did not have high salaries, and financial pressures were often acute (Howe 26-29; Langhans, "Actresses" 3-5). The backstage areas of the theatre were public meeting places where men of the court mixed with the performers. Not surprisingly, many actresses, already isolated from traditional family structures in which they were defined as daughters or wives, became involved in sexual relationships with some of these men. Actresses criticized for sexual relations outside marriage were in a problematic position. In public, they did exert some control over their lives and reputations, but the roles they played, which could be limited by typecasting and by stereotypical characterizations, affected their public *personae*. In general, they had relatively little control in sexual relationships with men of high rank.[18]

The seventeenth-century conflation of actress and prostitute further clarifies responses to *The Rover* in particular, to Behn's plays in general, and to her position as a writer. Actresses, like prostitutes, were defined as "public women" and criticized for using their bodies to earn money. Without a clearly defined place in the patriarchal family structure, actresses had to improvise new positions for themselves as public women. Like them, Behn earned her living in the public world, and was exposed to public criticism for behaviour which was acceptable for men. Some critics have suggested that Behn's sympathetic portrayals of prostitutes may indicate that she identifies her position with theirs, particularly in *The Rover*, in which the prostitute Angellica Bianca shares her initials, AB (Diamond 536; Todd *Sign* 1). In the "Postscript" to *The Rover*, a defence against charges that she plagiarized Thomas Killigrew's *Thomaso*, Behn asserts that "the only stolen object is the sign of Angellica," a reference to the three portraits which the courtesan Angellica Bianca hangs in the public square to attract customers in both *Thomaso* and *The Rover*. Elin Diamond suggests that the signs "may... constitute Behn's authorial signature" (536).

But if Behn meant to identify herself with Angellica Bianca, it was a controversial and ambiguous move. Jeslyn Medoff notes that Matthew Prior, who first identified Behn with Angellica Bianca, suggested the writer could "describe the cunning of a Jilting Whore" from experience (quoted Medoff 34). Robert Gould addressed a satire to Behn which concluded, "For Punk and Poetess agree so Pat,/You cannot be This and not be That" (quoted Diamond 520). These hostile seventeenth-century identifications of Behn with her prostitute character obviously have different aims than do more sympathetic recent discussions. Catherine Gallagher argues that Behn consciously "introduced to the world of English letters the professional woman writer as a newfangled whore" (66) in order to explore the simultaneous liberty and confinement the stage offered women. But the suggestion that the woman writer and the prostitute occupy similar cultural positions is not explicit in all of Behn's work. Indeed, the many prefaces in which she criticizes the double standards applied to her as a woman writer suggest that rather than wishing to be identified with her prostitute characters, Behn was eager to be judged by the same standards as male writers.

Ironically, there were already conventions in place which required women in the theatre to mask as men. The introduction of actresses to the English stage eliminated the practice of boys playing women's roles,[19] but the fascination with crossdressing was so deeply ingrained in pre-Restoration theatrical practice, that it resurfaced in what is known as the "breeches part." This is an adaptation of the female-page plot device found in many Elizabethan and Jacobean plays in which a woman character, played by a boy actor, is disguised as a boy. In many of the Restoration comedies which include the motif of the "breeches part", there is little plot motivation for the disguise, and minimal self-consciousness or reflection on the part of the character who disguises.

Behn frequently employs the convention; in *The Rover*, for example, Hellena appears in boy's clothes. Frances M. Kavenik suggests that Behn employed "breeches parts" in her plays to show that "women could share the libertine philosophy with men and experience its liberating effects, in much the same way as she was able to compete on relatively equal terms with the best male playwrights of her time" (190-91). Kavenik's optimistic assessment of Behn's ability to be accepted as a typical playwright is not shared by commentators who see the crossdressed female figure's relation to masculine and feminine as problematic. Crossdressing implies the transgression of boundaries which are traditionally regarded as fixed; Behn's plea for acceptance of "my masculine part, the Poet" demonstrates her awareness of the difficulty of acceptance. Jessica Munns suggests that as a writer Behn "double-dresses, and insists that her audience/readers accept her female gender and her right to a freedom of expression and range of topics hitherto limited to male literary production" ("Double Right" 195). The critical debate over the implications of Behn's anomalous place as a woman playwright frequently returns to the similarities of actress, prostitute, and writer as public women, and to the ways in which Behn's situation can be illuminated by comparison with the public women for whom and about whom she wrote.

Behn's last years, in which she produced many of her fictional prose narratives, were marked by illness and poverty, but also by tremendous productivity. The cause of her death is not known. She is buried in the cloister of Westminster Abbey under a plain black stone which inscribes her date of death as April 16, 1689, and commemorates her with the lines:

> Here lies a proof that wit can never be
> Defence enough against mortality.

Sources of *The Rover*

Like many other Restoration dramatists who relied on the body of plays written before 1642 for plot ideas and character types that could be adapted for contemporary audiences,[20] Behn was often inspired by earlier plays. Since she was writing for a specific and well-defined courtly audience, it is not surprising that her plays conformed to fashions in contemporary drama. But while the dramatic genres Behn employed were familiar,[21] she presented conventional dramatic situations from unusual perspectives.

The Rover falls into the general category of Restoration comedy, which relies on sexual innuendo, intrigue, and wit. More specifically, the play has been categorized as one of the last "sex comedies" popular in the 1670s (Scouten and Hume 56). These comedies often focus on the rake, or libertine, who criticizes marriage as an institution which controls sexuality and pleasure in the interest of property. But *The Rover* has links with a number of other genres and styles. It employs many of the conventions of Spanish comedy, which is characterized by complicated plots full of intrigue and disguise in which an imprisoned girl wins the right to choose her lover or husband (Burns 15). In addition, *The Rover* draws on early seventeenth-century comic genres. As we shall see, Behn adapts a model from Shakespeare's *As You Like It* to structure the relationships between women in the high and low plots. In the "Postscript" to *The Rover*, Behn acknowledges a debt to

Richard Brome's comic play *The Novella* (1632). But the most important source for *The Rover* is Thomas Killigrew's *Thomaso, or The Wanderer*, published in 1663 and probably written in the mid-1650s. Many of the episodes in *The Rover* are adaptations of scenes from Killigrew's play, which is in turn indebted to earlier texts, including Thomas Middleton's citizen comedy *Blurt Master Constable* (1601), Ben Jonson's *Volpone* (1607) and others.[22] *Thomaso* is a long, episodic prose drama which Killigrew seems to have planned to produce, but for which no records of performance exist. The hero of *Thomaso*, like its author, is a royalist supporter of the future Charles II who was exiled to Europe during the interregnum, the period when England was ruled by Parliament under Oliver Cromwell. Behn takes so many ideas for plot, setting, and action from *Thomaso*, that she feels obliged to defend herself against charges that the play "was *Thomaso* altered... That I have stolen some hints from it, may be a proof that I valued it more than to pretend to alter it" ("Postscript" to *The Rover*).

Behn's response here is ingenuous, for a great deal of the situation and plot material in *The Rover* is derived from *Thomaso*. However, she adds dramatic form to Killigrew's rambling and often unfocussed ten-act play, which Alfred Harbage has called "about the least stageworthy of Killigrew's productions" (102). In contrast, Behn's five-act play shows sophisticated dramatic structure and stagecraft. She certainly took more from *Thomaso* than her "Postscript" acknowledges. Yet *The Rover* also displays some of Behn's characteristic preoccupations, in particular the perspectives of women characters on love and marriage. In Killigrew's play, a romantic heroine named Serulina evades a repressive brother and several would-be rapists before she is married to the man of her choice, Thomaso the Wanderer. But the romantic heroine is not central to the play, for much of the action focusses on the sexual adventures of a group of exiled English cavaliers, including Thomaso, with women who include the prostitutes Angellica Bianca, a courtesan willing to experiment with a free love relationship with Thomaso, and Lucetta. Later, Thomaso rejects the female libertine's way of life to marry the virginal Serulina.[23]

In *The Rover* Behn shifts the focus from male to female characters. She develops the character of Angellica Bianca to illustrate the problematic position of a prostitute who has a place in society as long as she treats herself as a commodity but who is marginalized if she succumbs to romantic love. In the interplay between high and low plots, the play illustrates the similarities in the positions of prostitutes and marriageable young women. Behn splits Killigrew's romantic heroine Serulina into two sisters — Florinda, who resembles Serulina, and Hellena, a witty heroine who pursues the man of her choice and wins him as a husband. Behn also adds a cousin, Valeria, who becomes active in the plot late in the play. By doubling the lovers in the high plot, Behn contrasts the romantic and relatively passive "serious" lovers with the playful and witty lovers Hellena and Willmore. Thomaso, a complicated character who is alternately romantic and rakish, is split into two psychologically simpler characters: Belvile, and Willmore the Rover, who is less introspective than is Killigrew's Wanderer.

While *Thomaso* criticizes, from the perspective of the male characters, the economic structures which regulate sexuality, Behn is concerned with many of the same issues from the point of view of women characters.[24] In adapting Killigrew's plot in a way which clarifies the sexual double standards with which women struggle, she draws on the structural and thematic patterns of Shakespeare's *As You Like It*. In each play a pair of women characters who are confidantes and companions resist the power of male family members over them. The more independent woman character disguises herself as a boy, and in disguise develops a witty relationship with the man she loves. The quieter woman character has a more conventional, romantic relationship. Yet while she relies on characters and situations developed by Shakespeare, Behn makes a number of modifications. In *As You Like It* there is an accepted and unexamined class distinction between the women characters of the high and low plots. In *The Rover* Behn stresses the class distinctions between virgins and prostitutes, and many of the women characters discuss the paradoxes and double binds of gender and economic relations. The divisions between virgins and prostitutes have great social force. Angellica, the prostitute who tries to revise her place in the class/gender structure, is excluded by all characters from the marriages at the end of the play. By insisting on marriage, the virginal Hellena returns to the traditional institutions she criticized at the beginning. In *The Rover* the ideologies surrounding class and gender, and the conventions of the comic genre, require virgins and wives to remain in separate worlds from prostitutes.

The Rover

The Rover, Behn's most successful play, skilfully incorporates intrigue, disguise and slapstick into a complicated plot which ends in marriage. The central male character Willmore, the Rover, is a rake or libertine, a familiar dramatic type.[25] The rake, who exists outside the structures and mores of organized society, seeks liberty and pleasure; he often makes explicit criticisms of the institution of marriage because it suppresses sexual desire by incorporating it into the economic system. The heroine and rake are attracted to each other's love of pleasure and wit. In the fifth-act conversion typical of the genre, she persuades him to marry her in spite of his former critique of marriage as an institution.

One of the unusual elements of *The Rover* is that it presents issues usually introduced by the rake from the perspective of women characters. *The Rover* opens with a discussion by virginal women of their positions in the marriage economy. (The scene includes Hellena's vivid speech describing the disgust of a young woman at the thought of consummating a forced marriage to an older man.) Later Angellica Bianca argues that wives and prostitutes have much in common, in that they are treated as commodities in a system in which women are objects of economic exchange. In plot, structure, and characterization, the early parts of the play expose the sexual double standards by which women are judged, but these inherent contradictions in sexual and economic relations are blunted by setting and plot development.

Setting the play in Naples in the 1650s, Behn evokes a non-specific "exotic" foreign setting and places the events in a misty past. By 1677, the royalist cavaliers who had been in exile twenty years earlier were established as Tories in England; in retrospect, the instability and poverty of the interregnum is transformed into cheerful bohemianism. Willmore, the Rover, is a romanticized and comic figure of the libertine cavalier, seen from a nostalgic distance. (The character was so popular with contemporary audiences that Behn wrote a sequel in 1681, *The Second Part of The Rover*.)

As the early scenes make clear, there are three options for women in the society represented in *The Rover* — marriage, the convent, or prostitution. Marriages are arranged by fathers or brothers for their own political or financial benefit — in *The Rover* Florinda's brother Pedro tries marry Florinda to his own friend rather than to their father's candidate for her husband. After marriage, the wife moves from being controlled by the men of her family to being controlled by her husband. Hellena's description of Florinda's future role as a wife dwells on her confinement in the country and in the bedroom. Hellena's own fate is to become a nun. The nun's position, like the wife's, is arranged by her family, and has some elements in common with marriage — she is given a dowry to take to the convent, where she is called a bride of Christ. In the play, Hellena characterizes the nun's life by images of confinement such as the grate and the cell.

The young women conclude their discussions of their oppressed and confined situations in an act of resistance — they go out in disguise to join the carnival celebrations which are in progress.[26] Since everyone wears costumes and masks at carnival, Florinda disguises herself in a generic carnival habit, while Hellena becomes a gypsy. The anonymity made possible by carnival disguise functions, temporarily, to free the young women from the family. Disguise drives the plot in many ways, and gives the characters opportunities to meet the men they will marry at the end of the play. After first appearing as a gypsy, Hellena adopts the conventional "breeches part" when she appears as a boy, a disguise which is not anticipated in previous discussions. Hellena's ease with male disguise follows the Restoration theatrical convention of the "breeches part," which the heroine uses not as a way to examine gender roles but as a means to an end. Hellena does not mention any strategies needed to play a male convincingly, but exploits the possibilities of the disguise without drawing attention to it. As a boy, she brings messages to Willmore from his beloved (herself); her observations of Willmore's actions function to give her insight into his character, though she makes no explicit acknowledgment that she has learned anything else as a result of her crossgender roleplay. But in dressing as a boy, Hellena avoids some of the problems encountered by masked women, for she is not, as they are, constantly approached for sex.

The mask is a powerful image in Restoration drama.[27] In the 1660s, some women began to wear masks when they attended the theatre. But when prostitutes also began to wear masks, the distinctions between prostitutes and "respectable women" became blurred. The mask became a sign of the prostitute, but a sign which, with its offer of anonymity, could offer some freedom from conventional roles for any woman who wore it; Lesley Ferris suggests that the experience of wearing masks might have been not only "liberating" but also "subversive" (74).

In *The Rover* masks are often both subversive and liberating for the women characters; on the other hand, they also place some of the women in dangerous situations because of the association of the mask with the prostitute. The difficulty of distinguishing between "respectable women" and prostitutes is a recurrent theme in the play, and is made explicit in the first carnival scene, which opens with a group of exiled English royalists meeting in the streets of Naples. The English cavaliers watch in amusement as masked women pass by wearing, pinned to their clothing, papers which say, "Roses for every month." Belvile glosses the signs to mean, "They are, or would have you think, they're courtesans, who here in Naples are to be hired for the month." Belvile's awareness that the women may be courtesans, or may merely be masquerading as courtesans, prepares for a number of discussions and situations in which the parallels between "respectable women" and prostitutes as commodities are represented. So frequently is this subject articulated that Elin Diamond has suggested that Behn's theme in *The Rover* is "the commodification of women in the marriage market" (524).[28] The play stresses the ways in which the prostitute's economic position parallels that of the wife's in the patriarchal family. A prostitute who has a protector or a pimp is enclosed in a structure in which her place as commodity is stable and recognizable. At the beginning of the play Angellica Bianca is alone, her previous protector having died. She is actively looking for a replacement, rich enough to pay her a thousand crowns a month. The economic relationship between courtesan and protector parallels that between husband and wife, yet its temporary aspect gives Angellica more control than a wife. Angellica is able to choose her purchaser — something that women who are destined to be wives do not always have the power to do. And it is Angellica who makes explicit the similarities between the situations of wife and prostitute in the long scene in which she and Willmore debate the relationships between love and money. Angellica eloquently deplores the double standards employed by men, but she is affected by Willmore's critique of her as a mercenary; her attraction to him induces her to agree to bypass the usual exchange of money for sex in the interests of an ideal of free love.

Angellica, like the virgins of the play, is subject to what her servant and advisor Moretta calls the "disease of our sex," romantic love. Love, like a disease, weakens Angellica. When she succumbs to Willmore's argument that love ought to be given rather than sold, she gives up her independence and becomes vulnerable both emotionally and economically. She not only gives herself to Willmore, but she gives him money also. Having gained this prize, Willmore immediately shifts his attention to the pursuit of Hellena, whom he has previously met in her gypsy disguise.

While it is against Willmore's principles of free love to marry, at the end of the play he abrogates these principles in order to marry the witty virgin Hellena, something he would not do for the prostitute Angellica. Driven by jealousy and unrequited love, Angellica threatens Willmore with a pistol, but she is easily disarmed by Antonio, Willmore's rival for possession of her. As a result of her vulnerability to romantic love, Angellica Bianca moves from a position of strength in an economic system which recognizes her value as a commodity to a position of dependence in an economy of emotion. After she falls in love, she changes from an articulate and intelligent character, aware of the ways in which economic and sexual systems interact to control women, to a stereotype of the jealous and emotional woman. Ultimately, she is a melodramatic figure who is written out of the play and hustled offstage before the questions she has raised can be fully resolved.

If Angellica is the clichéd whore with a heart (though not of gold), the other prostitute, Lucetta, is a mercenary "jilting wench." When she robs and humiliates Blunt, who has believed her to be attracted to him, his anger unleashes his hatred of all women. Prostitutes who are mercenary, like Lucetta, may gain money and keep control, but they bring the rage of their victims on other women. At several points the plot shows men's resentment against prostitutes, and when the boundaries between prostitutes and "respectable" women are blurred, all women become potential targets of rage.

The vulnerability of women who are not under the protection of men is represented at numerous points in *The Rover* by attempted rapes.[29] Florinda, the prototypical romantic heroine, is especially targetted. Before the play begins she is rescued by Belvile from soldiers invading Pamplona. During the play she is twice threatened with rape. When she is waiting for Belvile in the garden at night, the drunken Willmore stumbles into her and argues that since her garden gate was open, she must have meant to entice him. She is rescued by Belvile and Frederick, who condemn Willmore for drunkenness and bungling but not for his violent struggle with Florinda. Later, when Florinda is escaping her brother she runs into Belvile's house wearing carnival disguise and mask. The only person present is Blunt, bitterly angry at his betrayal by Lucetta, and determined to beat and to rape the next woman he sees. While Blunt is threatening Florinda, Frederick returns and amusedly decides to join Blunt. Florinda persuades the men to delay their proposed rape by giving them a diamond and promising to prove her identity as a respectable woman. The jewel makes Frederick pause, since he does not want "to be taken for raping a maid of quality when we only mean to ruffle a harlot." Later, virtually all the male characters, including Florinda's brother, draw swords for the first chance at her. Although Belvile arrives, he cannot think of a way to stop the men from chasing her around the room without revealing her identity to her brother. Florinda is saved not by her fiancé, but by the wit of her cousin Valeria. When her identity as a respectable woman betrothed to Belvile is revealed, her future husband's friends make only perfunctory apologies, and Florinda does not seem to expect more.

The difficulty Blunt and Frederick have in telling a "maid of quality" from a "harlot" is shared by all the men in the play. Blunt mistakes the prostitute Lucetta for a rich wife who loves him; Willmore mistakes Florinda for a prostitute; the masquerading women wear papers on their clothing "as if whores." The boundaries separating "woman of quality" and "whore" have been destabilized. Yet the implications of this instability are not developed. Angellica Bianca is emotionally weakened when she stops selling herself and gives herself for love, but the sympathy which the character begins to evoke is undercut when she becomes jealous and threatens violence. In the end, all the problems previously raised by Angellica are erased, since her challenge to Willmore is not resolved.

In this comedy, which, conventionally, ends in marriage, the figure of the prostitute cannot be integrated. Marriage is seen as a problem by the women of quality at the beginning of the play; by the end, marriage is a solution to a problem, though not an ideal one. Hellena pragmatically chooses marriage over Willmore's offer of free love because she recognizes that no matter how bad marriage might be, the hazard of being unmarried is greater. Sleeping with Willmore outside of marriage will lead, she argues, to "a pack of troubles and a cradle full of repentance"; to avoid it, she calls for "old gaffer Hymen" to regularize the union. Hellena's disguise has given her insight into Willmore's inconstancy, but her insistence on marriage seems less a strategy to control him than a way to protect herself from the consequences of being defined as a "whore."

Hellena's utilitarian attitude to marriage can be contrasted to that of Belvile and Florinda, who adhere to a romanticized view of woman as a prize to be won by a man's prowess. They first fall in love after Belvile saves her at the siege of Pamplona; later Belvile fights a duel in disguise and wins Florinda again. When he asserts, "She's mine by conquest, sir, I won her by the sword" he speaks not to her but to her brother; the focus is not on his love for her or her choice of him, but on his skill at winning a wife. The early parts of the play define him as a protector of his beloved, yet no character comments on Belvile's ineffectual presence when Florinda is being chased by his friends. The third marriage, that of Valeria and Frederick, is a conventional dramatic one, the result of an immediate attraction which has not been analyzed or tested. No explicit attention is drawn to the problematic nature of any of these marriages, except perhaps in the final couplet, which refers to "the storms o' the marriage bed."

Critical appraisals of *The Rover*, like other developments in Behn criticism, have until recently focussed on her life. Frederick Link's survey of Behn's body of work (1968) concisely categorizes and summarizes her many literary productions. Since the early 1980s there has been a noticeable increase in critical discussions, though many of these studies still have a primary interest in Behn's professional and sexual life. Most of the criticism is devoted to her fiction, with a decided focus on *Oroonoko*. A rapidly growing critical debate on her poetry has been encouraged by the publication of Germaine Greer's edition of *The Uncollected Verse of Aphra Behn* (1989) and Janet Todd's edition of Behn's *Poetry* (1992). Behn's plays are often considered briefly in general discussions of women writers or Restoration drama. A relatively small but rapidly growing body of criticism analyzes individual plays, especially *The Lucky Chance*, *The Widow Ranter*, and *The Rover*. Some insightful discussions of *The Rover* are included in two recent anthologies, *Curtain Calls: British and American Women and the Theatre, 1660-1820*, edited by Mary Ann Schofield and Cecilia Macheski (1991) and *Rereading Aphra Behn: History, Theatre and Criticism*, edited by Heidi Hutner (1993).

Critical responses to *The Rover* generally acknowledge that there are a number of tensions and contradictions inherent in the play. In their discussions of the extent to which the play criticizes its society, critics give different emphasis to the beginning of the play and its conclusion, to the explicit and the implicit, and to conventional and unconventional elements. The plot includes duels, robberies, and attempted rapes; characters make casual antisemitic slurs; anticatholic comments acknowledge the inquisition in the background. Laura Brown argues that "the form implies a condemnation of that very society whose standards constitute the terms of its action" (61), while Jessica Munns suggests that the content, not the form, is the source of social criticism, when she mentions "uncomfortable moments that throw off-balance the move to a happy ending" ("Double Right" 201.) The "uncomfortable moment" most often discussed is Angellica's final scene in which she threatens Willmore with a pistol, a scene which Link suggests does "not quite fit the comic world of the play" (*Rover* Introduction xvi). Other "uncomfortable moments" include antisemitic slurs used in conversation[30] as well as the proposed rapes of Florinda, but these problems are rarely explored in criticism of the play.

Another concern is how to define and understand Behn's unusual portrayal of male and female characters. Some critics prefer to define her as a proto-femininist or feminist writer (Langdell 110). However, this perspective is qualified by arguments such as Nancy Cotton's that she represents male libertine characters much less critically than do Etherege and Wycherly ("Pattern Hero" 215-218). While Cotton suggests that Behn's interest in writing "from her own gender perspective" ("Pattern Hero" 217) might account for these relatively uncritical male representations, their characterizations put into question the seriousness with which we are to interpret the women characters' criticisms of marriage. The women's complaints about marriage focus on their own places in the social structure; male control of the institution is not emphasized so much as the position of women as pawns within it. The play opens with a sympathetic portrayal of women subject to male control, but there is throughout an indulgent tolerance of individual male characters. Although all of the men except Belvile propose rape, not even the women criticize the practice. Blunt's angry and explicit statements of his desire to beat and to rape women in revenge for his treatment by Lucetta are incongruous elements in a character who is introduced as a dim-witted comic butt. And Willmore's drunkenness and pursuit of all women are represented as endearing foibles. (Belvile does criticize Willmore, primarily for his tendency to interfere drunkenly with Belvile's secret meetings with Florinda.) While Willmore makes many speeches attacking mercenary relationships, his practice is not as honourable as his arguments would suggest. He may not be explicitly seeking a rich woman, but when he finds one he does not hesitate to exploit her financial resources.[31]

Cotton's argument that Behn "seems unconcerned about these masculine doubts" ("Pattern Hero" 217) implies that Behn is more interested in the women than the men. Alternately, the relatively unproblematic portrayal of Willmore and the other male characters might be interpreted as part of a realistic or unsentimental representation of a culture characterized by violence and discrimination. The violent setting can also be seen as exotic local colour introduced by a playwright who knows what her audience wants.[32] Whether or not *The Rover* is most striking for its protofeminist perspective on women characters in which, as Jaqueline Pearson argues, "images of female power are...most emphatic" (154) or is characterized by "a restoration of patriarchal authority" (Hutner 103),[33] its many tensions and contradictions make it a fascinating play.

Stage History

The first recorded production of *The Rover* was at the Dorset Garden Theatre on 24 March 1677, though it is not known if this was the premiere of the play (*London Stage* 1:256). The play was very popular in the London theatre for almost eighty years. It was presented at court in 1680, 1685, 1687, and 1690, was performed in London theatres virtually every year until 1743, and remained in the repertoire until 1757.

The first edition of the play, published in 1677, includes a cast list which names a number of popular actors. The two co-managers of the theatre, Thomas Betterton (1635-1710) and William Smith (died 1695), had key roles. Betterton, who played the romantic Belvile, was famous as an actor and manager. Mary Betterton, née Saunderson (c. 1637-1712) performed Florinda, Belvile's beloved.

William Smith took the role of Willmore, the Rover. Though Smith's name is not now as famous as Betterton's, he was a respected actor whose first documented appearance on the London stage was as Antonio in *The Duchess of Malfi* in 1662. Hellena was one of Elizabeth Barry's (c. 1658-1713) early roles — she later became famous, particularly for creating leading roles in the tragedies of Thomas Otway. Blunt was performed by the comedian Cave Underhill (c. 1634-c.1710). This was a popular role for Underhill; he performed some of Blunt's scenes in a booth at Greenwich as late as 1710 (*Dictionary of National Biography*).

The key part of Angellica Bianca was played by Mrs. Anne Quin (fl. 1660-1683), who had earlier appeared as Mrs. Anne Marshall. The first cast list, which was reproduced in many later editions, including the 1915 Montague Summers' edition, assigns the part of Angellica Bianca to "Mrs. Gwin," and many records indicate that Nell Gwyn herself played the role.[34] But since Anne Quin is variously identified in contemporary records and cast lists as Mrs Quin, Quinn, Quyn, Guin, Gwin and Wyn, not surprisingly there has been some confusion of the two actresses. Although Nell Gwyn had performed in some of Behn's early plays, and Behn had dedicated *The Feigned Courtesans* to her in 1679, Gwyn left the stage after 1671, six years before *The Rover* was produced.

The choice of Anne Quin for Angellica Bianca is interesting, since it seems that she had also been Killigrew's choice for the role in a planned production of Behn's source for *The Rover, Thomaso, or The Wanderer. Thomaso* was published in 1663, after Killigrew acquired the patent for the Bridges Street Theatre, but without prologue, epilogue, or actors' names in the list of *dramatis personae*, suggesting that it had not been acted before publication. *The London Stage* suggests that when Killigrew was manager of the King's Company he "prepared *Thomaso* for production in the autumn of 1664," with an intended cast that included Mrs. Anne Marshall (later Quin) as Angellica Bianca and Nell Gwyn as Paulina, but that "no notice of production exists" (1:84). *A Biographical Dictionary of London Actors* suggests that Quin "probably" acted the role in *Thomaso* (12:243). When Behn wrote *The Second Part of the Rover* in 1681, apparently by popular demand, several of the original cast reprised their roles as Anne Quin may have done between *Thomaso* and *The Rover*. It was common practice for performers in sequels to play the same characters they had created (Holland 67). Cave Underhill again played Blunt, and Smith played the romantic cavalier Willmore for the second time. Fittingly, it was his first role after returning from military service in an army that supported James II after his abdication in 1688. In following an exiled Stuart king, Smith's life seems to have imitated his character's.

Elizabeth Barry could not reprise the important role of Hellena in *The Second Part of The Rover*, since that character has died; early in Act 1 of *Rover 2*, Willmore briefly mentions his wife's death at sea. Willmore, however, is not changed by marriage or by Hellena's death, for he is soon pursuing a courtesan named La Nuche, played by Barry. In *Rover 2* the love affair between Willmore and the courtesan is more "successful" for Willmore since his arguments in favour of free love, made to Angellica Bianca and then to Hellena in *The Rover*, are accepted by La Nuche, who at the end of the play pledges herself to live with him in spite of poverty and risk. There is no character analogous to Hellena, who points out in *The Rover* the extent to which an ideal of free love carries many possible costs for women which are not borne by men.[35] While many Restoration playwrights had close connections with the companies for which they wrote their plays and knew the actors with whom the play would be cast, it is difficult to be sure what control Behn might have had over the casting of Barry as La Nuche. Assuming that she "took care over the repeated casting," Peter Holland argues that the audience's

> perception of underlying structure, the inevitability of a match between Smith and Mrs. Barry, is allowed to carry over between the parts. Mrs. Behn can profit from this to underline the alternatives: Willmore is forced to marry Hellena but his bargain with La Nuche is achieved without marriage — a reflection of the degradation of the heroine into a prostitute. . .

and of the increasingly extra-social position of the
rake in the comedies of the 1680s. (67-68)

Like many sequels, *The Second Part of the Rover* was not as
successful as the original had been, nor does it seem to have
been performed after its first production in 1681.

There are indications that some of the situations in *The
Rover* were increasingly seen as risqué, particularly after
Jeremy Collier's *Short View of the Immorality and Profaneness of
the English Stage* in 1698 helped to define, as well as to en-
courage, changing standards in language and situations considered appropriate for theatrical representation. A prompt-
book of the first edition of *The Rover*, which Edward A.
Langhans believes dates from the 1720s, indicates a number
of cuts of sexually explicit lines and episodes (144-148).
Scouten and Hume note that in the 1750s and 1760s there
were many hostile attacks on what they call "the older comedies" by "*writers who attended the theatre and supported the
drama*" (79; their emphasis), and that in the 1760s and 1770s
many of these plays were performed only in altered versions
(80).

A report in *The London Chronicle* (22-24 February, 1757)
of a production of *The Rover* at Covent Garden illustrates the
shift in audience response. The ladies in the theatre "are first
alarmed; then the Men stare: The Women put up their Fans"
when "One of the Personages of the Drama takes off his
Breeches in the Sight of the Audience," a reference to the
scene in which Blunt undresses in Lucetta's chamber. The account goes on to note that the play was written "in the disso-
lute Days of Charles the Second; and that Decency at least is,
or ought to be, demanded at present" (quoted Agate 21).
Montague Summers' account of the same production, which
he dates as 19 February 1757, stresses that Mr. Shuter, the actor playing Blunt, did not improvise new and more shocking
business here, but "exactly followed the old realistic traditions and in Act III as the business requires he undressed to
his very shirt and drawers" (190). Summers adds that in the
scene in which Blunt climbs from the sewer the actor "re-
sorted to the original methods and covered himself with
chawed gingerbread" (191). Perhaps it was the faithfulness of

this production to stage tradition, and its distance from the increasingly popular sentimental drama, which made it seem inappropriate in 1757. This is the last recorded performance of *The Rover* in London until 1790, when John Philip Kemble presented a revision of the play called *Love in Many Masks*.

Kemble's alterations of *The Rover* indicate that the play was increasingly seen as morally suspect. Kemble shortened the five acts to three, and in the process cut out much of the dialogue and action pertaining to sex. Hellena's speech about the horror of forced marrage is removed, and the rape plot against Florinda is merely implied. Hellena makes some very highminded speeches about honour ("My birth, my breeding and pride raise me far above the coarse interchange of mere convenient pleasures — I offer my heart for yours" [*Love in Many Masks* 23]). Like Hellena, Willmore is more refined and calm than he is in *The Rover*; in particular, he is less often drunk and chasing women, hence more worthy of a woman like Hellena. The Blunt episodes are also softened; Lucetta's trap door drops him into another street, rather than into the sewer, and she tells her colleagues that she is trying to teach him a lesson about vanity, an ostensibly moral purpose absent from Behn's play. The final lines of Kemble's version substitute optimism about marriage and honour for Willmore's cynicism about "the storms o' th' marriage bed."

Love in Many Masks is a much simpler and politer play than *The Rover*. Although the production, and some individual performances, were praised for their humour, a newspaper review published 9 March 1790 nevertheless complains that "the ideas are constantly indelicate, and the language frequently gross". The reviewer especially objects to a play with a courtesan as a central character, and suggests that the adapter ought to have eliminated Angellica Bianca entirely.[36] *Love in Many Masks* was performed only a few times; it had eight performances in March 1790 and one in October of that year. After Kemble's failed attempt to present the play in a relatively sanitized version, *The Rover* virtually disappeared from the stage until the late 1970s.

Most of the few recent productions of *The Rover* have been by university or small alternative theatre groups; the exception is the Royal Shakespeare Company's revival in 1986 of an adapted version. A review of a production at the University of Illinois at Chicago Circle in 1979 praises the company for stressing physicality over a conventional comedy of manners style (Hume 412-13); the Folger Theatre Group's production in Washington in 1982 was deemed "surprisingly sophisticated" (Gusso, *NYT* Jan 14, 1982:C17). The play was also performed by the Upstream Theatre in London in July 1984 (Carlson 152-154).

For its production at the Swan Theatre in 1986 and then at the Mermaid Theatre in London in 1987, the RSC director and adaptor John Barton incorporated some passages from Killigrew's *Thomaso*. Barton changed the setting of the play to the West Indies, making an explicit link between sexual double standards and slavery not found in the Behn text. He also added numerous lines in which women characters explicitly express sexual desire. While the production received generally favourable reviews, some academic commentators have been less approving of Barton's interpolations from Killigrew and his other alterations of Behn's text. Nancy Copeland argues that the passages from Killigrew function to represent relationships between men and women "more crudely than in Behn's play" ("Reproducing *The Rover*" 51), in particular by making Angellica Bianca "a conventional, and therefore easily recognizable, prostitute figure" ("Reproducing *The Rover*" 52). Jessica Munns suggests that "in seeking recognition of Behn's relevance for today, Barton obscures the points at which we can find genuine parallels between Behn's texts and our social contexts... [and] obscures the points at which Behn's values and moral patterns are not our own" ("Barton" 19; see also Carlson 155-56). An American production of *The Rover* at the Williamstown Theatre Festival followed the RSC innovation of setting the play in the West Indies and altering the text; the reviewer found the second half "tedious" (Rev. Frank Rich *NYT* July 27, 1987:C18).[37]

While *The Rover* may be returning to the theatrical repertoire, the Royal Shakespeare Company's decision not to perform it without interpolation and revision suggests that the play continues to have the power to challenge conventional expectations. The successful revivals of Behn's text, however, indicate that *The Rover* still has the potential to reward production.

Notes

1. Many discussions of Behn's sexuality and relationship with Hoyle use her novels and poetry as evidence of her inner life, but do not problematize the relationship between art and life. Hoyle was involved in several duels, was charged and acquitted of sodomy, and ultimately killed in a knife fight. Most of Behn's biographers, including Sackville-West, Woodcock, Duffy, Goreau and Mendelson read Behn's *Love-Letters to a Gentleman* (1684) as autobiographical records of her relationship with Hoyle, and must therefore speculate whether he was homosexual or bisexual. See also Salvaggio's suggestion that Behn's heterosexual desire "is undermined by the homosexual and/or homosocial" (257).

2. For a discussion of Behn's literary reputation in the seventeenth and eighteenth centuries, see Medoff (33-35).

3. Herst's play was produced at Tarragon Theatre in Toronto in April 1992 and at the University of Guelph, Ontario, 29 November to 4 December 1993.

4. Most biographies give a probable birthdate of 1640, partly because a now discredited baptismal reference to an Aphra Amis born in that year was once thought to be Behn's. However, Duffy strongly argues for 1640 (Duffy 16-23) while Mendelson believes that references to Behn's youth at the time of the voyage to Surinam mean that she cannot have been born before the late 1640s (116). In a recent article, Jane Jones agrees with Duffy that Behn was "likely" born to Bartholomew Johnson and Elizabeth Denham in 1640 in Harbledown, near Canterbury (290).

5. Behn's poems are often read singly and autobiographically. For example, many critics read "The Disappointment" as a poem about Behn's dismay at a male lover's impotence, while Arlene Stiebel interprets Behn's "To the Fair Chlorinda, who

made Love to me, Imagin'd More than Woman" as evidence that Behn is a "lesbian author" (161-163).

6. The biographies disagree greatly on the significance of many fragments of information, but I do not analyze these disputes in detail, since my focus is on the parts of Behn's life and dramatic career which are documented, especially those which are relevant to a reading of *The Rover*.

7. Because no second edition is extant, some bibliographers cast doubt on its designation. W.J.Cameron discusses the "Memoir" in *New Light on Aphra Behn* (14-17; 87-100). For a detailed discussion of the differences between subsequent versions of the early biographical accounts of Behn see Robert Adams Day, "Aphra Behn's First Biography."

8. The relevant part of Culpepper's memoir is reproduced by Mendelson (116). Duffy relies on this document in her discussion of Behn's birth (19), as does Jones, while Mendelson argues that it is inaccurate (116). See also Goreau's discussion (11-13).

9. Hargreaves' "A Case for Mr. Behn" is the most specific defence of the existence of a husband. Goreau argues that since there are no records attacking Behn's right to call herself Mrs. Behn, she was probably known by her contemporaries to have been married (85). No documentary evidence is known which would support the theory that "Mr. Behn" died in the plague.

10. Scot, a political exile, had military associations with the Dutch army. All of Behn's recent biographers discuss Behn's rumoured relationship with Scot in Surinam and her dealings with him in Antwerp. Todd and McKee draw on unpublished letters of Thomas Corney, another English agent, to outline some of the intrigue and double dealing in which Behn was involved. They conclude that Behn's mission was less important – and less secret – than she thought (Todd and McKee 4-5).

11.   These letters, held at the Public Record Office, are transcribed by Cameron (34-86). Goreau concisely summarizes and annotates them (90-112).

12.   It is not known precisely how many plays Behn wrote, since several anonymous plays are attributed to her and several titles attributed to her have been lost; sixteen plays are extant.

13.   After *The Forced Marriage, or The Jealous Bridegroom* the Dorset Garden Theatre produced *The Amorous Prince, or The Curious Husband* (1671); *The Dutch Lover* (1673); *The Town Fop, or Sir Timothy Tawdry* (1676) and *Abdelazar, or The Moor's Revenge*, a tragedy (1676). Two anonymous plays of 1677 have been attributed to Behn, *The Debauchee, or The Credulous Cuckold* and *The Counterfeit Bridegroom, or The Defeated Widow* (Stanton 340-41).

14.   For a brief survey of unfavourable opinions of Behn's "immoral" subject matter see Hutner ("Introduction" to *Rereading* 2).

15.   Playwrights were paid the proceeds from the third day's performance of a play.

16.   Two of Katherine Philips' heroic dramas were produced in the 1660s, and Francis Boothby and Elizabeth Polwhele each had one play produced, but none of the three defined herself as a professional writer.

17.   Nicoll notes with surprise that Mary Sanderson, the actress who married the actor Thomas Betterton, had no scandal attached to her name (71). The Sanderson/Betterton marriage prefigures the many professional and marital partnerships which characterized the British theatre in the eighteenth and nineteenth centuries, including those of the Garricks, Siddons, Kembles, and Keans.

18. A case in point is an actress named Rebecca Marshall, who was kidnapped by a courtier in spite of appealing to the king for protection (Howe 33; Goreau 160).

19. However not all crossdressing disappeared; male actors continue to caricature older women in what are now known as "dame parts."

20. Many of Shakespeare's plays were revised between 1660 and 1690; the works of Beaumont and Fletcher, and of Thomas Middleton, as well as other playwrights, were also favourite sources for adaptations in the late seventeenth century.

21. Behn's prose works are more innovative in terms of genre than her plays. In particular *Oroonoko* and *Love Letters* are by many critics seen as prescient precursors of the novel. See, for example, Janet Todd's discussion in *The Sign of Angellica* (76-83).

22. Behn's ambiguous reference to Brome in the "Postscript" may be designed to suggest that Killigrew also drew on Brome. For Killigrew's sources, see Alfred Harbage (119-222), who briefly discusses Killigrew's debts to Calderon's *La Dama Duende* (180, n. 4; 221) as well as to John Fletcher's *The Captain* and Ben Jonson's *Volpone* (221-22). Harbage also discusses autobiographical elements in *Thomaso* (102; 106-7;116).

23. See Harold Weber's discussion of Thomaso as rake and Angellica as female libertine (153-61).

24. For a general analysis of Behn's revision of Killigrew see Jones DeRitter. Nancy Copeland focusses on Behn's treatment of Killigrew's women characters ("Once a Whore"). See also Heidi Hutner's interesting discussion of "the resistance of the 'other' body" in both parts of *The Rover*.

25. The rake's place in Restoration drama of this period is discussed in detail by Harold Weber.

26. Mark Lussier briefly sketches some of the ways in which theoretical discussion of the carnivalesque might be applied to *The Rover* ("Marrying" 231-32); see Terry Castle for a more developed theoretical framework of the carnivalesque in Restoration and eighteenth-century literature.

27. The importance of the mask is central to most discussions of Restoration drama. For a brief outline of the function of the mask see Bevis 71-72. For a description of masquerade costumes and an analysis of the importance of the masquerade in eighteenth-century society, see Terry Castle, *Masquerade and Civilization* (chapters 1 and 2).

28. Lussier develops Diamond's argument when he suggests that "women are consumable commodities who circulate within a masculine economy of desire" ("Marrying" 234). See also Lussier's discussion of Behn's use of economic language in her later plays *The City Heiress* and *The Feigned Courtesans* ("Vile Merchandize").

29. Discussions of the frequency of rape as a plot motif in Restoration drama tend to focus on tragedy and heroic drama. See Susan Staves' discussion of rape as property crime in heroic drama (59, 259) and Jean I. Marsden on the relation of rape and chastity in Restoration adaptations of Shakespeare (52-54). Elizabeth Howe discusses Restoration rape scenes as "voyeurism" (43-49).

30. *The Rover* is not the only play in which Behn employs conventional antisemitic stereotypes; in *The Second Part of the Rover* two women characters named in the *Dramatis Personae* as a monster and a dwarf are described to Willmore as "two Jewish Monsters arriv'd from Mexico, Jews of vast Fortunes, with an old Jew Uncle their Guardian" (Summers, *Works of Aphra Behn* 1: 124).

31. Willmore takes gold from Angellica, though he returns it when she threatens him with a pistol. At the beginning of *The Second*

Part of The Rover he notes that Hellena died after a few months of marriage, and that her large dowry is already spent.

32. Seventeenth-century audiences seem to have consistently focused on Willmore and Blunt as favourite characters. Hellena dies before the opening of the sequel in which Willmore's drinking, sexual adventures and complicated intrigues are the centre of the plot.

33. Hutner argues that patriarchal authority which is restored at the end of the first part of *The Rover* is undercut in the sequel ("Revisioning").

34. Genest asserts that Nell Gwyn acted at Dorset Garden Theatre, (1:210); other sources, including the *Dictionary of National Biography*, also indicate that Nell Gwyn played Angellica Bianca. For a discussion of the confusion between Anne Quin and Nell Gwyn see *A Biographical Dictionary of London Actors* (12:244).

35. Nancy Cotton argues that in *The Rover* Angellica Bianca "loses" Willmore to Hellena because she is "humourless" (*Women Playwrights* 65); but that La Nuche in *The Second Part of the Rover* is able to "win" Willmore because she "has the wit and sense of humour that Angellica Bianca lacked" (*Women Playwrights* 67). In assessing the trajectory of Behn's comedies at this point in her career, Cotton suggests that "In each case, the more generous woman gets the man" (*Women Playwrights* 67). See also Heidi Hutner's analysis of the two parts of *The Rover* in relation to Killigrew's *Thomaso*.

36. Unidentified clipping of 9 March 1790, in file on *Love in Many Masks* held at Covent Garden Theatre Museum Library.

37. The play was also produced by the Revels Players at the University of Illinois in Champaign-Urbana in April 1990 (rev. *Daily Illini* 18 April, 1990), and at the Union Theatre in Peterborough, Ontario, February 1-6, 1994.

Selected Bibliography

References to secondary sources cited in the "Introduction" are listed under "Sources," as are some other useful works relating to Behn. Adaptations of *The Rover*, some recent editions of *The Rover*, and other works by Behn are listed under the heading "Adaptations and Modern Editions of Behn's Works."

Early editions of *The Rover* which I have consulted for this edition are briefly described in "A Note on the Text," and are listed at the beginning of the "Textual Notes" immediately following the play.

Modern Editions and Adaptations of Behn's Works

Behn, Aphra. *An Adaptation of The Rover: A Programme/Text With Commentary by Simon Trussler*. Swan Theatre Plays. London: Methuen with Royal Shakespeare Company, [1987].

——. *Five Plays: The Lucky Chance, The Rover Part 1, The Widow Ranter, The False Count, Abdelazer*. Introduced by Maureen Duffy. London: Methuen, 1990.

——. *Oroonoko, or The Royal Slave*. Ed. Adelaide P. Amore. Lanham, MD: University Press of America, 1987.

——. *Oroonoko, The Rover and Other Works*. Ed. Janet Todd. Harmondsworth: Penguin, 1992: 155-248.

——. *The Rover*. Ed. Frederick M. Link. Regent's Restoration Drama Series. Lincoln: University of Nebraska Press, 1967.

——. *The Rover* in *The HBJ Anthology of Drama*. Ed. W.B. Worthen. Fort Worth: Harcourt Brace Jovanovich, 1993: 321-353

——. *The Works of Aphra Behn. Volume I: Poetry*. Ed. Janet Todd. Columbus: Ohio State University Press, 1992.

——. *The Rover* in *Restoration Comedy*. Ed. A. Norman Jeffares. 4 vols. London: Folio Press, 1974: vol. 2: 230-331.

——. *The Works of Aphra Behn*. Ed Montague Summers. 6 vols. London: 1915. New York: Phaeton, 1967.

——. *The Uncollected Verse of Aphra Behn*. Ed. Germaine Greer. Stump Cross, Essex: Stump Cross, 1989.

Kemble, J.P *Love in Many Masks*. London: 1790.

Sources

Agate, James, ed. *The English Dramatic Critics, An Anthology: 1660-1932*. London: Arthur Barker, [1932].

Armistead, J.M. *Four Restoration Playwrights: A Reference Guide to Thomas Shadwell, Aphra Behn, Nathaniel Lee, and Thomas Otway*. Boston: G.K. Hall, 1984.

Bevis, Richard W. *English Drama: Restoration and Eighteenth Century, 1660-1789*. London and New York: Longman, 1988.

A Biographical Dictionary of Actors, Actresses, Musicians, Dancers, Managers and Other Stage Personnel in London, 1660-1800. Ed. Philip H. Highfill Jr., Kalman A. Burnim and Edward A. Langhans. 14 vols. Carbondale and Edwardsville: Southern Illinois University Press, 1973-

Brown, Laura. *English Dramatic Form, 1660-1760: An Essay in Generic History*. New Haven and London: Yale University Press, 1981.

Burns, Edward. *Restoration Comedy: Crises of Desire and Identity*. New York: St. Martin's Press, 1987.

Cameron, W.J. *New Light on Aphra Behn*. Auckland: University of Auckland Press, 1961.

Carlson, Susan. *Women and Comedy: Rewriting the British Theatrical Tradition.* Ann Arbor: University of Michigan Press, 1991.

Castle, Terry. *Masquerade and Civilization: The Carnivalesque in Eighteenth-Century English Culture and Fiction.* Stanford: Stanford University Press, 1986.

Copeland, Nancy. "'Once a whore and ever'? Whore and Virgin in *The Rover* and its Antecedents". *Restoration* 16:1 (Spring 1992): 20-27.

——. "Reproducing *The Rover*: John Barton's *Rover* at the Swan." *Essays in Theatre* 9:1 (Nov. 1990): 45-59.

Cotton, Nancy. "Aphra Behn and the Pattern Hero" in *Curtain Calls: British and American Women and the Theatre, 1660-1820.* Ed. Mary Anne Schofield and Cecilia Macheski. Athens: Ohio University Press, 1991: 211-219.

——. *Women Playwrights in England c. 1363-1750.* Lewisburg: Bucknell University Press; London and Toronto: Associated University Presses, 1980.

Day, Robert Adams. "Aphra Behn's First Biography." *Studies in Bibliography* 22 (1969): 227-40.

DeRitter, Jones. "The Gypsy, *The Rover*, and the Wanderer: Aphra Behn's Revision of Thomas Killigrew." *Restoration* 10:2 (Fall 1986): 82-92.

Diamond, Elin. "Gestus and Signature in *The Rover*." *ELH* 56:3 (Fall 1989): 519-41.

Duffy, Maureen. *The Passionate Shepherdess: Aphra Behn 1640-89.* London: Jonathan Cape, 1977.

Ferris, Lesley. *Acting Women: Images of Women in Theatre.* New York: New York University Press, 1989.

Gallagher, Catherine. "Who Was That Masked Woman? The Prostitute and the Playwright in the Comedies of Aphra Behn" in *Rereading Aphra Behn: History, Theory, and Criticism.* Ed. Heidi Hutner. Charlottesville and London: University Press of Virginia, 1993: 65-85. Previously published in *Women's Studies* 15 (1988): 77-83 and in *Last Laughs: Perspectives on Women and Comedy.* Ed. Regina Barreca. New York: Gordon and Breach, 1988.

Gardiner, Judith Kegan. "Aphra Behn: Sexuality and Self-respect." *Women's Studies* 7 (1980): 67-78.

Genest, John. *Some Account of the English Stage, From the Restoration in 1660 to 1830.* 10 vols. 1832. New York: Burt Franklin, [1965].

Goreau, Angeline. *Reconstructing Aphra: A Social Biography of Aphra Behn.* New York: Dial, 1980.

Gussow, Mel "Stage: *The Rover,* of 17th Century," Review of *The Rover* by Aphra Behn. Folger Theatre Group, Washington. *New York Times,* January 14, 1982: C17.

Harbage, Alfred. *Thomas Killigrew Cavalier Dramatist 1612-83.* 1930. New York: Benjamin Blom, 1967.

Hargreaves, H.A. "A Case for Mr. Behn." *Notes and Queries* June 1962: 203-205.

——. "Mrs. Behn's Warning of the Dutch 'Thames Plot'." *Notes and Queries* February 1962: 61-63.

Hobby, Elaine. *English Women's Writing 1646-1688.* London: Virago, 1988.

Holland, Peter. *The Ornament of Action: Text and Performance in Restoration Comedy.* Cambridge: Cambridge University Press, 1979.

Howe, Elizabeth. *The First English Actresses: Women and Drama 1660-1700.* Cambridge: Cambridge University Press, 1992.

Hume, Robert D. "Revision of *The Rover.*" University of Illinois, Chicago Circle. *Theatre Journal* 31:3 (Oct. 1979): 412-413.

Hutner, Heidi, ed. *Rereading Aphra Benn: History, Theory and Criticism.* Charlottesville: University Press of Virginia, 1993.

—. "Revisioning the Female Body: Aphra Behn's *The Rover* Parts I and II" in *Rereading Aphra Behn: History, Theory, and Criticism.* Ed. Heidi Hutner. Charlottesville and London: University Press of Virginia, 1993: 102-120.

Jerrold, Walter and Clare Jerrold. "Aphra Behn: The Incomparable Astraea" in *Five Queer Women.* London: Brentano's, 1929: 1-82.

Jones, Jane. "New Light on the Background and Early Life of Aphra Behn." *Notes and Queries* N.S. 37:3 (Sept. 1990): 288-292.

Kavenik, Frances M. "Aphra Behn: the Playwright as 'Breeches Part'" in *Curtain Calls: British and American Women and the Theatre, 1660-1820.* Ed. Mary Anne Schofield and Cecilia Macheski. Athens: Ohio University Press, 1991: 177-192.

Killigrew, Thomas. *Thomaso, or The Wanderer* in *Comedies and Tragedies.* London: 1664.

Langbaine, Gerard. *An Account of the English Dramatick Poets.* 1691. 2 vols. Los Angeles: William Andrews Clark Memorial Library, University of California, 1971.

Langdell, Cheri Davis. "Aphra Behn and Sexual Politics: A Dramatist's Discourse With Her Audience" in *Drama, Sex and Politics.* Ed. James Redmond. Themes in Drama. London: Cambridge University Press, 1985: 109-128.

Langhans, Edward A. "Three Early Eighteenth-Century Promptbooks." *Theatre Notebook* 20 (Summer 1966): 142-150.

——. "Tough Actresses to Follow" in *Curtain Calls: British and American Women and the Theatre, 1660-1820.* Ed. Mary Anne Schofield and Cecilia Macheski. Athens: Ohio University Press, 1991: 3-17.

Link, Frederick M. *Aphra Behn.* New York: Twayne, 1968.

The London Stage 1660-1800: A Calendar of Plays, Entertainments & Afterpieces Together with Casts, Box-receipts and Contemporary Comment Compiled from the Playbills, Newspapers and Theatrical Diaries of the Period. Part 1, 1660-

1700. Ed. William van Lennep. Carbondale: University of Illinois Press, 1960-

Lussier, Mark. "'Marrying that Hated Object': The Carnival of Desire in Behn's *The Rover*" in *Privileging Gender in Early Modern England*. Ed Jean R. Brink. *Sixteenth-Century Essays & Studies*, Vol. XXIII. Kirksville, Missouri: Sixteenth Century Journal Publishers, 1993: 225-39.

_____. "'The Vile Merchandize of Fortune': Women, Economy and Desire in Aphra Behn." *Women's Studies* 18 (1991): 379-393.

Marsden, Jean I. "Rewritten Women: Shakespearean Heroines in the Restoration" in *The Appropriation of Shakespeare: Post-Renaissance Reconstructions of the Work and the Myth*. Ed. Jean I. Marsden. New York: St. Martin's, 1991: 43-56.

Medoff, Jeslyn. "The Daughters of Behn and the Problem of Reputation" in *Women, Writing, History 1640-1740*. Ed. Isobel Grundy and Susan Wiseman. Athens: University of Georgia Press, 1992: 33-54.

Mendelson, Sara Heller. "Aphra Behn" in *The Mental World of Stuart Women: Three Studies*. Brighton: Harvester, 1987: 116-184.

Munns, Jessica, "Barton and Behn's *The Rover*: or, The Text Transpos'd." *Restoration and Eighteenth Century Theatre Research*, 2nd series 3:2 (Winter 1988): 11-22.

——. "'Good, Sweet, Honey, Sugar-Candied Reader': Aphra Behn's Foreplay in Forewords" in *Rereading Aphra Behn: History, Theory, and Criticism*. Ed. Heidi Hutner. Charlottesville and London: University Press of Virginia, 1993: 44-64.

——. "'I By A Double Right Thy Bounties Claim': Aphra Behn and Sexual Space" in *Curtain Calls: British and American Women and the Theater, 1660-1820*. Ed. Mary Ann Schofield and Cecilia Macheski. Athens: Ohio University Press, 1991: 193-210.

Nicoll, Allardyce. *Restoration Drama 1660-1700*. Vol. 1 of *A History of English Drama 1660-1900*. 6 vols. 4th ed. Cambridge: Cambridge University Press, 1955.

O'Donnell, Mary Ann. *Aphra Behn: An Annotated Bibliography of Primary and Secondary Sources*. New York: Garland, 1986.

Payne, Deborah C. "'And Poets Shall by Patron-Princes Live': Aphra Behn and Patronage" in *Curtain Calls: British and American Women and the Theater, 1660-1820*. Ed. Mary Ann Schofield and Cecilia Macheski. Athens: Ohio University Press, 1991: 105-119.

Pearson, Jacqueline. *The Prostituted Muse: Images of Women and Women Dramatists 1642-1737*. New York: St. Martin's, 1988.

Platt, Harrison Gray Jr. 'Astrea and Celadon: An Untouched Portrait of Aphra Behn," *PMLA* 49 (1934): 544-59.

Rich, Frank. "Stage: *The Rover*, Feminist Comedy From 1677". Review of *The Rover* by Aphra Behn. Williamstown Theater Festival, Williamstown. *New York Times*, July 27, 1987: C18.

Sackville-West, V. *Aphra Behn: The Incomparable Astraea*. New York: Viking, 1928.

Salvaggio, Ruth. "Aphra Behn's Love: Fiction, Letters and Desire" in *Rereading Aphra Behn: History, Theory, and Criticism*. Ed. Heidi Hutner. Charlottesville and London: University Press of Virginia, 1993: 253-272.

Schofield, Mary Ann and Cecilia Macheski, eds. *Curtain Calls: British and American Women and the Theater, 1660-1820*. Athens, Ohio University Press, 1991.

Scouten, Arthur H. and Robert D. Hume "'Restoration Comedy' and its Audience" in *The Rakish Stage: Studies in English Drama*. Ed. Robert D. Hume. Carbondale and Edwardsville: Illinois University Press, 1983: 46-81.

Southerne, Thomas. *Oroonoko*. Ed. Maximilian E. Novak and David Stuart Ross. Lincoln: University of Nebraska Press, 1976.

Stanton, Judith Philips. "'This New-Found Path Attempting': Serious Plays by Women on the London Stage 1660-1737" in *Curtain Calls: British and*

American Women and the Theater, 1660-1820. Ed. Mary Ann Schofield and Cecilia Macheski. Athens: Ohio University Press, 1991: 325-356.

Staves, Susan. *Players' Sceptres: Fictions of Authority in the Restoration*. Lincoln and London: University of Nebraska Press, 1979.

Stiebel, Arlene. "Not Since Sappho: The Erotic in Poems of Katherine Philips and Aphra Behn" in *Homosexuality in Renaissance and Enlightenment England: Literary Representations in Historical Context*. Ed. Claude Summers. Binghamton, NY: Harrington Park Press; New York: Haworth, 1992: 153-171.

Summers, Montague. *The Restoration Theatre*. London: Kegan Paul, Trench, Trubner, & Co., 1934.

Todd, Janet and Francis McKee. "The 'Shee Spy'; Unpublished letters on Aphra Behn, Secret Agent." *Times Literary Supplement*, September 10, 1993:4-5.

Todd, Janet. *The Sign of Angellica: Women, Writing and Fiction, 1660-1800*. London: Virago, 1989.

Ward, Charles E. *The Letters of John Dryden With Letters Addressed to Him*. 1942. New York: AMS, 1965.

Weber, Harold. *The Restoration Rake-Hero: Transformations in Sexual Understanding in Seventeenth-Century England*. Madison: University of Wisconsin Press, 1986.

Woodcock, George. *Aphra Behn: The English Sappho*. Montreal: Black Rose, 1989. Prev. pub. as *The Incomparable Aphra*. London: Boardman, 1948.

A Note on the Text

The first edition of *The Rover* was a quarto published in 1677, the year the play was first produced. The second edition was also published in quarto in 1697. The play appears in collected editions of Behn's works published in 1702 and 1724; a third quarto was published in 1709. The copytext for this edition of *The Rover* is the first edition of 1677, which is coherent and includes many detailed stage directions; it exists in three issues, described in detail by Mary Ann O'Donnell (32-38); see also Frederick Link (*Rover* ix-x). These three issues are illuminating for what they tell us about Behn's acknowledgment of authorship. Although the title pages of the first two issues do not name the author, the "Prologue" of all three issues refers to the author as "he". The third issue, however, adds "written by Mrs. A. Behn" to the title page. In some copies of the second issue, and in the third issue the author's "Postscript" is printed with the addition of the phrase "especially of our sex", an acknowledgment that the author is a woman.

I have collated copies of the first edition held by the British Library and the Thomas Fisher Rare Book Library at the University of Toronto with a microfilm of the Huntington Library copy. In addition, I have collated the British Library copies of the second and third quartos, and of the first two collected editions. In a few instances I have adopted readings from editions other than the first. These cases are indicated in the Textual Notes following the play. I have also consulted editions of *The Rover* by Montague Summers (1915), Frederick Link (1967), Norman Jeffares (1974) and Janet Todd (1992).

Spelling and capitalization have been modernized, and the many typefaces used in early editions, such as italic type for proper names within speeches, have been simplified. Long "s" is printed as "s"; ampersands are expanded to "and". When a contraction in the 1677 text has no effect on pronunciation, as when "'d" represents a silent "ed" ending, modern spelling is used. (For example, "shock'd" is changed to "shocked".) However, when a contraction suggests pronunciation, I have preserved its spelling, as, for example, "'twill" for "it will", "for't" for "for it", "e'er" for "ever", "'tis" for "it is", etc. When different spellings of a word are used in the first edition, I have regularized them. In the 1677 edition, for example, "pistol" and "pistole" are used interchangeably to signify either a gun or a coin; I use "pistol" for the gun, and "pistole" for the coin. The regularized form "'sheartlikins" is used for the variants "sheartlikins", "'dsheartlikins", "adsheartlikins" and "adshartlikins" which appear in the 1677 edition. As well, I have retained a few non-standard spellings which suggest pronunciation, such as "learnt" for "learned". In a few cases spelling in the 1677 edition is ambiguous; I have recorded the variants in the Textual Notes.

Although most of *The Rover* is written in prose, the play includes a few songs and verses. There are also some sententious or sentimental speeches which in the early editions have been set as poetry, and which are often metrically irregular. I have retained these passages as poetry. Textual notes are indicated by a dagger (†).

The first edition of *The Rover* includes detailed stage directions. A double-dagger (‡) indicates stage directions I have added.

As much as possible, I have retained the punctuation of the 1677 edition. The many dashes, run-on sentences and sentence fragments evoke energetic, colloquial speech, suggesting how lines might have been delivered on the seventeenth-century stage. While I have punctuated some extremely long sentences with semi-colons and full stops, my aim has been been to alter the rhythms of the speeches as little as possible.

THE ROVER

PROLOGUE

Wits, like physicians, never can agree,
When of a different society.
And Rabel's Drops were never more cried down
By all the learned doctors of the town,
Than a new play whose author is unknown.   5
Nor can those doctors with more malice sue
(And powerful purses) the dissenting few,
Than those with an insulting price do rail
At all who are not of their own cabal.

    If a young poet hit your humour right,   10
You judge him then out of revenge and spite.
So amongst men there are ridiculous elves,
Who monkeys hate for being too like themselves.
So that the reason of the grand debate,
Why wit so oft is damned, when good plays take,   15
Is that you censure as you love, or hate.

    Thus like a learned conclave poets sit,
Catholic. judges both of sense and wit,
And damn or save, as they themselves think fit.
Yet those who to others' faults are so severe,   20
Are not so perfect but themselves may err.
Some write correct† *indeed, but then the whole*
(Bating their own dull stuff i'th' play) is stole;
As bees do suck from flowers their honey dew,
So they rob others striving to please you.   25

    Some write their characters gentle† *and fine,*
But then they do so toil for every line,
That what to you does easy seem, and plain,
Is the hard issue of their labouring brain.
And some th'effects of all their pains we see,   30
Is but to mimic good extempore.
Others by long converse about the town,

---

3 Rabel's Drops] a patent medicine
9 cabal] clique
17 conclave] meeting to elect a pope; private meeting
18 catholic] universal; broadminded

Have wit enough to write a lewd lampoon,
But their chief skill lies in a bawdy song.
In short, the only wit that's now in fashion,   35
Is but the gleanings of good conversation.
As for the author of this coming play,
I asked him what he thought fit I should say
In thanks for your good company today:
He called me fool, and said it was well known   40
You came not here for our sakes, but your own.
New plays are stuffed with wits, and with debauches,[†]
That crowd and sweat like cits, in May-Day coaches.

Written by a Person of Quality..

---

38 him] the first edition of *The Rover* was published anonymously; the writer of the
    "Prologue" here speaks as if the author is a man. See "Introduction" for a discussion
    of Behn's situation as a woman writer and her acknowledgement of authorship.
43 cits] citizens; a derogatory term used by the leisured classes to refer to merchants and
    tradespeople concentrated in the City of London
43 May-Day coaches] It was the custom to ride around Hyde Park in coaches on May Day;
    possibly an urban variation on traditional May Day expeditions to the countryside.
44 Person of Quality] Prologues and Epilogues of Restoration plays were often
    contributed by someone other than the author of the play.

THE ACTORS' NAMES.

Mr. Jevon[†]	Don Antonio,	The Viceroy's son.	
Mr. Medbourne[†]	Don Pedro,	A noble Spaniard, his friend.	
Mr. Betterton	Belvile,	An English colonel in love with Florinda.	
Mr. Smith	Willmore,	The ROVER.	5
Mr. Crosby[†]	Frederick,	An English gentleman and friend to Belvile and Blunt.[†]	
Mr. Underhill	Blunt,	An English country gentleman.	
Mr. Richards	Stephano,	Servant to Don Pedro.	10
Mr. Percival[†]	Phillippo,	Lucetta's gallant.	
Mr. John Lee	Sancho,	Pimp to Lucetta.	
	Biskey, and Sebastian,	Two bravoes to Angellica.	
	Officers and Soldiers.		15
	Diego[†] Page To Don Antonio.		
	Boy		

---

5 Rover] wanderer; also pirate
13 bravoes] hired soldiers; bodyguards

Women.

Mrs. Betterton	Florinda,	Sister to Don Pedro.	20
Mrs. Barry[†]	Hellena,	A gay young woman designed for a nun, and sister to Florinda.	
Mrs. Hughes	Valeria,	A kinswoman to Florinda.	
Mrs. Quin[†]	Angellica Bianca,	A famous courtesan.	25
Mrs. Leigh	Moretta,	Her woman.	
Mrs. Norris	Callis,	Governess to Florinda and Hellena.	
Mrs. Gillow[†]	Lucetta,	A jilting wench.	
	Servants,		30
	Other Masqueraders,		
	Men and Women.		

The Scene: NAPLES, in Carnival time.

---

34 Naples] Although the play is set in Naples, numerous traces of the the Spanish setting
   of *Thomaso* (Behn's source) remain in *The Rover*.
34 Carnival] pre-Lenten festival in which people wear costumes

The
ROVER

OR, The Banished Cavaliers.

What is love?

ACT the First.
Scene the First. A Chamber.

Enter Florinda and Hellena.

FLORINDA.

What an impertinent thing is a young girl bred in a nunnery!   1
How full of questions! Prithee no more Hellena; I have told thee
more than thou understand'st already.

HELLENA.

The more's my grief. I would fain know as much as you, which
makes me so inquisitive; nor is't enough I know you're a lover,   5
unless you tell me too, who 'tis you sigh for.

FLORINDA.

When you're a lover, I'll think you fit for a secret of that nature.

HELLENA.

'Tis true, I never was a lover yet — but I begin to have a shrewd
guess what it is to be so, and fancy it very pretty to sigh, and sing,
and blush, and wish, and dream, and wish, and long and wish to   10
see the man, and when I do, look pale and tremble; just as you
did when my brother brought home the fine English colonel to
see you — what do you call him, Don Belvile?

Title: Cavaliers] Supporters of the English monarchy during the English civil war period.
Many cavaliers left England after the execution of King Charles I in 1649.

FLORINDA

Fie, Hellena.

HELLENA

That blush betrays you — I am sure 'tis so — or is it Don Antonio 15
the viceroy's son? Or perhaps the rich old Don Vincentio whom
my father designs you for a husband? Why do you blush again?

FLORINDA

With indignation, and how near soever my father thinks I am to
marrying that hated object, I shall let him see I understand better
what's due to my beauty, birth and fortune, and more to my soul, 20
than to obey those unjust commands.

HELLENA

Now hang me if I don't love thee for that dear disobedience. I
love mischief strangely, as most of our sex do, who are come to
love nothing else — but tell me dear Florinda, don't you love that
fine Anglese? For I vow, next to loving him myself, 'twill please 25
me most that you do so, for he is so gay and so handsome.

FLORINDA.

Hellena, a maid designed for a nun ought not to be so curious in
a discourse of love.

HELLENA

And dost thou think that ever I'll be a nun? Or at least till I'm so
old, I'm fit for nothing else — faith no, sister; and because I hope 30
he has some mad companion or other that will spoil my devotion, nay I'm resolved to provide myself this carnival, if there be
e'er a handsome proper fellow of my humour above ground,
though I ask first.

FLORINDA

Prithee be not so wild. 35

HELLENA

Now you have provided yourself of a man, you take no care for
poor me — prithee tell me, what dost thou see about me that is
unfit for love — have I not a world of youth? A humour gay? A
beauty passable? A vigour desirable? Well shaped? Clean limbed?
Sweet breathed? And sense enough to know how all these ought 40
to be employed to the best advantage? Yes, I do and will; therefore lay aside your hopes of my fortune by my being a devote,

---

25 Anglese] Englishman

and tell me how you came acquainted with this Belvile, for I perceive you knew him before he came to Naples.

FLORINDA

Yes, I knew him at the siege of Pamplona;[†] he was then a colonel 45
of French horse, who when the town was ransacked, nobly
treated my brother and myself, preserving us from all insolences;
and I must own (besides great obligations) I have I know not
what that pleads kindly for him about my heart, and will suffer
no other to enter — but see, my brother. 50

Enter Don Pedro, Stephano with a masquing habit, and Callis.

PEDRO

Good morrow sister — pray, when saw you your lover Don Vincentio?

FLORINDA

I know not, sir — Callis, when was he here? For I consider it so little, I know not when it was.

PEDRO

I have a command from my father here to tell you you ought not 55
to despise him, a man of so vast a fortune and such a passion for
you — Stephano, my things.

Puts on his masquing habit.

FLORINDA

A passion for me, 'tis more than e'er I saw, or he had a desire
should be known — I hate Vincentio, sir, and I would not have a
man so dear to me as my brother follow the ill customs of our 60
country, and make a slave of his sister — and sir, my father's will
I'm sure you may divert.

PEDRO

I know not how dear I am to you, but I wish only to be ranked in
your esteem equal with the English Colonel[†] Belvile — why do

---

42 devote] a nun or religious person
45 Pamplona] a fortified town in Navarre
Stage Direction: masquing habit] costume worn at carnival

you frown and blush? Is there any guilt belongs to the name of   65
that cavalier?

FLORINDA.

I'll not deny I value Belvile. When I was exposed to such dangers
as the licensed lust of common soldiers threatened, when rage
and conquest flew through the city – then Belvile, this criminal
for my sake, threw[†] himself into all dangers to save my honour,   70
and will you not allow him my esteem?

PEDRO.

Yes, pay him what you will in honour – but you must consider
Don Vincentio's fortune, and the jointure he'll make you.

FLORINDA.

Let him consider my youth, beauty and fortune, which ought not
to be thrown away on his age and jointure.   75

PEDRO.

'Tis true, he's not so young and fine a gentleman as that Belvile –
but what jewels will that cavalier present you with? Those of his
eyes and heart?

HELLENA.

And are not those better than any Don Vincentio has brought
from the Indies?   80

PEDRO.

Why, how now! Has your nunnery breeding taught you to understand the value of hearts and eyes?

HELLENA.

Better than to believe Vincentio's deserve value from any woman
– he may perhaps increase her bags, but not her family.

PEDRO.

This is fine – go – up to your devotion; you are not designed for   85
the conversation of lovers.

HELLENA.   [*Aside.*]

Nor saints yet a while,[†] I hope.

– Is't not enough you make a nun of me, but you must cast my
sister away too, exposing her to a worse confinement than a religious life?   90

---

73 jointure] part of a marriage settlement which provides for a wife's support after her
    husband's death
84 bags] wealth

PEDRO.

The girl's mad — it is a confinement to be carried into the country, to an ancient villa belonging to the family of the Vincentios these five hundred years, and have no other prospect than that pleasing one of seeing all her own that meets her eyes — a fine air, large fields, and gardens where she may walk and gather flowers.

HELLENA.

When, by moonlight? For I am sure she dares not encounter with the heat of the sun; that were a task only for Don Vincentio and his Indian breeding, who loves it in the dog days — and if these be her daily divertisements, what are those of the night? To lie in a wide moth-eaten bed chamber, with furniture in fashion in the reign of King Sancho the First; the bed, that which his forefathers lived and died in.

PEDRO.

Very well.

HELLENA.

This apartment (new furbished and fitted out for the young wife) he (out of freedom) makes his dressing room, and being a frugal and jealous coxcomb, instead of a valet to uncase his feeble carcass, he desires you to do that office — signs of favour I'll assure you, and such as you must not hope for, unless your woman be out of the way.

PEDRO.

Have you done yet?

HELLENA.

That honour being past, the giant stretches itself, yawns and sighs a belch or two, loud as a musket, throws himself into bed, and expects you in his foul sheets, and ere you can get yourself undressed, calls you with a snore or two — and are not these fine blessings to a young lady?

PEDRO.

Have you done yet?

---

99 Indian breeding] presumably Don Vincentio was born in the Indies
99 dog days] hottest days of summer
100 divertisements] diversions
105 new furbished] refurbished

more witty etc. than Florinda.

HELLENA.

And this man you must kiss; nay you must kiss none but him, too
— and nuzzle through his beard to find his lips. And this you
must submit to for threescore years, and all for a jointure.   120

PEDRO.

For all your character of Don Vincentio, she is as like to marry
him as she was before.

HELLENA.

Marry Don Vincentio! Hang me, such a wedlock would be worse
than adultery with another man. I had rather see her in the Hotel
de Dieu†, to waste her youth there in vows and be a handmaid to   125
lazars and cripples, than to lose it in such a marriage.

PEDRO.

You have considered, sister, that Belvile has no fortune to bring
you to — banished his country, despised at home, and pitied
abroad.

HELLENA.

What then? The viceroy's son is better than that old Sir Fifty.   130
Don Vincentio! Don Indian! He thinks he's trading to Gambo
still and would barter himself (that bell and bauble) for your
youth and fortune.

PEDRO.

Callis, take her hence, and lock her up all this Carnival, and at
Lent she shall begin her everlasting penance in a monastery.   135

HELLENA.

I care not; I had rather be a nun than be obliged to marry as you
would have me, if I were designed for't.

PEDRO.

Do not fear the blessing of that choice — you shall be a nun.

HELLENA.

Shall I so? You may chance to be mistaken in my way of devotion
— a nun! Yes, I am like to make a fine nun! I have an excellent   140
humour for a grate.

---

125 Hotel de Dieu] hospital run by nuns for the care of the destitute and outcast
126 lazars] people with Hansen's diseases (leprosy); more generally, diseased people
131 Gambo] Gambia, on the coast of Africa
141 grate] bars in the door of a convent, marking the separation of the nun from the
world

[*Aside.*] I'll have a saint of my own to pray to shortly, if I like any
that dares venture on me.

PEDRO.

Callis, make it your business to watch this wild cat. As for you
Florinda, I've only tried you all this while and urged my father's   145
will; but mine is that you would love Antonio. He is brave and
young, and all that can complete the happiness of a gallant maid.
This absence of my father will give us opportunity to free you
from Vincentio by marrying here, which you must do tomorrow.

FLORINDA.

Tomorrow!   150

PEDRO.

Tomorrow, or 'twill be too late — 'tis not my friendship to Antonio which makes me urge this, but love to thee and hatred to
Vincentio — therefore, resolve upon tomorrow.

FLORINDA.

Sir, I shall strive to do as shall become your sister.

PEDRO.

I'll both believe and trust you. Adieu.   155

Exeunt Pedro and Stephano.

HELLENA.

As becomes his sister! That is to be as resolved your way, as he is
his —

Hellena goes to Callis.

FLORINDA.

I ne'er till now perceived my ruin near.
I've no defence against Antonio's love,
For he has all the advantages of nature,   160
The moving arguments of youth and fortune.

HELLENA.

But hark you, Callis, you will not be so cruel to lock me up indeed, will you?

CALLIS.

I must obey the commands I have[†] — besides, do you consider
what a life you are going to lead?   165

HELLENA.

Yes, Callis, that of a nun; and till then I'll be indebted a world of
prayers to you if you'll let me now see what I never did, the divertisements of a carnival.

CALLIS.

What, go in masquerade? 'Twill be a fine farewell to the world, I
take it — pray, what would you do there?   170

HELLENA.

That which all the world does, as I am told — be as mad as the
rest and take all innocent freedoms. Sister, you'll go too, will you
not? Come, prithee be not sad. We'll outwit twenty brothers if
you'll be ruled by me — come, put off this dull humour with your
clothes, and assume one as gay, and as fantastic, as the dress my   175
cousin Valeria and I have provided, and let's ramble.

FLORINDA.

Callis, will you give us leave to go?

CALLIS. [*Aside.*]

I have a youthful itch of going myself. — Madam, if I thought
your brother might not know it, and I might wait on you; for by
my troth I'll not trust young girls alone.   180

FLORINDA.

Thou see'st my brother's gone already, and thou shalt attend,
and watch us.

Enter Stephano.

STEPHANO.

Madam,[†] the habits are come, and your cousin Valeria is dressed,
and stays for you.

FLORINDA.

'Tis well. I'll write a note, and if I chance to see Belvile, and want   185
an opportunity to speak to him, that shall let him know what I've
resolved in favour of him.

HELLENA.

Come, let's in and dress us.

Exeunt.

Scene II
A Long Street

Enter Belvile melancholy, Blunt and Frederick.

FREDERICK.
  Why† what the devil ails the colonel? In a time when all the world
  is gay, to look like mere Lent thus? Had'st thou been long
  enough in Naples to have been in love, I should have sworn some
  such judgment had befallen thee.

BELVILE.
  No, I have made no new amours since I came to Naples.   5

FREDERICK.
  You have left none behind you in Paris?

BELVILE.
  Neither.

FREDERICK.
  I cannot divine the cause then, unless the old cause, the want of
  money.

BLUNT.
  And another old cause, the want of a wench — would not that re-   10
  vive you?

BELVILE.
  You are mistaken, Ned.

BLUNT.
  Nay, 'sheartlikins, then thou'rt past cure.

FREDERICK.
  I have found it out; thou hast renewed thy acquaintance with the
  lady that cost thee so many sighs at the siege of Pamplona — pox   15
  on't, what d'ye call her — her brother's a noble Spaniard —
  nephew to the dead general — Florinda — ay Florinda — and will
  nothing serve thy turn but that damned virtuous woman? Whom
  on my conscience thou lovest in spite too, because thou seest little or no possibility of gaining her.   20

---

13 'sheartlikins] God's little heart; a "minced oath" combining "God's heart" and
  "bodikin." Also "heartikin," "adsheartlikins."

BELVILE.

> Thou art mistaken. I have interest enough in that lovely virgin's
> heart to make me proud and vain, were it not abated by the se-
> verity of a brother, who perceiving my happiness —

FREDERICK.

> Has civilly forbid thee the house?

BELVILE.

> 'Tis so; to make way for a powerful rival, the viceroy's son, who 25
> has the advantage of me in being a man of fortune, a Spaniard,
> and her brother's friend; which gives him liberty to make his
> court, whilst I have recourse only to letters and distant looks
> from her window, which are as soft and kind as those which
> heaven sends down on penitents. 30

BLUNT.

> Heyday! 'Sheartlikins, simile! By this light, the man is quite
> spoiled. Fred, what the devil are we made of that we cannot be
> thus concerned for a wench? 'Sheartlikins, our cupids are like the
> cooks of the camp, they can roast or boil a woman, but they have
> none of the fine tricks to set 'em off, no hogoes to make the 35
> sauce pleasant and the stomach sharp.

FREDERICK.

> I dare swear I have had a hundred as young, kind and handsome
> as this Florinda; and dogs eat me, if they were not as trouble-
> some to me i'the morning as they were welcome o'er night.

BLUNT.

> And yet I warrant he would not touch another woman if he 40
> might have her for nothing.

BELVILE.

> That's thy joy, a cheap whore.

BLUNT.

> Why 'sheartlikins, I love a frank soul — when did you ever hear of
> an honest woman that took a man's money? I warrant 'em good
> ones — but gentlemen, you may be free, you have been kept so 45
> poor with Parliaments and Protectors, that the little stock you

---

35 hogoes] piquant or strongly-flavoured mixtures used in cooking; relishes
46 Protectors] During the period of Parliamentary rule, Oliver Cromwell used the title of
   Protector of England.

have is not worth preserving — but I thank my stars, I had more grace than to forfeit my estate by cavaliering.

BELVILE.

Methinks only following the court, should be sufficient to entitle 'em to that.   50

BLUNT.

'Sheartlikins, they know I follow it to do it no good, unless they pick a hole in my coat for lending you money now and then, which is a greater crime to my conscience, gentlemen, than to the Commonwealth.

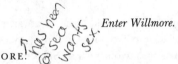 *Enter Willmore.*

WILLMORE.

Ha! Dear Belvile! Noble colonel!   55

BELVILE.

Willmore! Welcome ashore, my dear rover! What happy wind blew us this good fortune?

WILLMORE.

Let me salute. my dear Frederick and then command me. How is't, honest lad?

FREDERICK.

Faith, sir, the old complement, infinitely the better to see my   60
dear mad Willmore again. Prithee, why camest thou ashore? And where's the Prince?

WILLMORE.

He's well, and reigns still lord of the watery element. I must aboard again within a day or two, and my business ashore was only to enjoy myself a little this carnival.   65

---

48 cavaliering] During the protectorate, cavaliers who left England could have their estates confiscated. Blunt boasts that he has managed to travel overseas without identifying himself, or being identified, as a cavalier, and hence is not liable to lose his property.

49 court] of the exiled Prince Charles, later Charles II

54 Commonwealth] name for England during Parliamentary rule

58 salute] kiss

62 Prince] Prince Charles

Women want constancy and marriage
- men don't want commitment - they want sex.

BELVILE.

Pray know our new friend, sir; he's but bashful, a raw traveller,
but honest, stout and one of us.

Embraces Blunt.

WILLMORE.

That you esteem him gives him an interest here.

BLUNT.

Your servant, sir.

WILLMORE.

But well — faith, I'm glad to meet you again in a warm climate,   70
where the kind sun has its god-like power still over the wine and
women — love and mirth are my business in Naples, and if I mistake not the place, here's an excellent market for chapmen of
my humour.

BELVILE.

See, here be those kind merchants of love you look for.   75

*Enter several men in masquing habits, some playing on music, others
dancing after; women dressed like courtesans, with papers pinned on their
breasts, and baskets of flowers in their hands.*

BLUNT.

'Sheartlikins, what have we here?

FREDERICK.

Now the game begins.

WILLMORE.

Fine pretty creatures! May a stranger have leave to look and love?
What's here — [*Reads the papers.*] "Roses for every month"?

BLUNT.

"Roses for every month"? What means that?   80

BELVILE.

They are, or would have you think, they're courtesans, who here
in Naples, are to be hired by the month.

---

73 chapmen] merchants

WILLMORE.

Kind and obliging to inform us — pray, where do these roses grow? I would fain plant some of 'em in a bed of mine.

WOMEN.

Beware such roses, sir. 85

WILLMORE.

A pox of fear; I'll be baked with thee between a pair of sheets, and that's thy proper still; so I might but strew such roses over me, and under me — fair one, would you would give me leave to gather at your bush this idle month; I would go near to make some body smell of it all the year after. 90

BELVILE.

And thou hast need of such a remedy, for thou stink'st of tar and rope's ends, like a dock or pest-house.

The woman puts herself into the hands of a man and exeunt.

WILLMORE.

Nay, nay, you shall not leave me so.

BELVILE.

By all means use no violence here.

WILLMORE.

Death! Just as I was going to be damnably in love, to have her led 95 off! I could pluck that rose out of his hand, and even kiss the bed the bush grew in.

FREDERICK.

No friend to love like a long voyage at sea.

BLUNT.

Except a nunnery, Frederick.

WILLMORE.

Death! But will they not be kind? Quickly be kind? Thou know'st 100 I'm no tame fighter, but a rampant lion of the forest.

---

86 baked...still] Willmore's *double entendre* refers to the process by which rose petals are distilled to make rosewater.
92 pest-house] hospital for plague victims

Advance from the farther end of the scenes two men dressed all over with horns of several sorts, making grimaces at one another, with papers pinned on their backs.

BELVILE.

Oh the fantastical rogues, how they're dressed! 'Tis a satire against the whole sex.

WILLMORE.

Is this a fruit that grows in this warm country?

BELVILE.

Yes, 'tis pretty to see these Italians start, swell and stab at the   105
word "cuckold," and yet stumble at horns on every threshold.

WILLMORE.

See what's on their back — [*Reads*] "Flowers of every night."
Ah, rogue! And more sweet than "Roses of every month"! This is a gardener of Adam's own breeding.

They dance.

BELVILE.

What think you of those grave people? Is a wake in Essex half so   110
mad or extravagant?

WILLMORE.

I like their sober grave way; 'tis a kind of legal authorized fornication, where the men are not chid for't, nor the women despised, as amongst our dull English even the monsieurs want that part of good manners.   115

BELVILE.

But here in Italy a monsieur is the humblest, best-bred gentleman — duels are so baffled by bravoes, that an age shows not one but between a Frenchman and a hangman, who is as much too hard for him on the piazza, as they are for a Dutchman on the New Bridge. — but see, another crew.   120

Stage Direction: horns] sign of a cuckold
113 chid] chided
119 piazza] plaza or square
120 Dutchman on the New Bridge] a reference to the French defeat of the Dutch at Niuewerbrug in 1673.

Enter Florinda, Hellena and Valeria, dressed like gypsies; Callis and
Stephano; Lucetta, Phillipo and Sancho in masquerade.

HELLENA.

Sister, there's your Englishman, and with him a handsome
proper fellow — I'll to him, and instead of telling him his fortune,
try my own.

WILLMORE.

Gypsies, on my life — sure these will prattle if a man cross their
hands.   125

Goes to Hellena.

Dear, pretty (and I hope) young devil, will you tell an amorous
stranger what luck he's like to have?

HELLENA.

Have a care how you venture with me, sir, lest[†] I pick your
pocket, which will more vex your English humour than an Italian
fortune will please you.   130

WILLMORE.

How the devil cam'st thou to know my country and humour?

HELLENA.

The first I guess by a certain forward impudence, which does not
displease me at this time; and the loss of your money will vex you
because I hope you have but very little to lose.

WILLMORE.

Egad child, thou'rt i'th'right; it is so little, I dare not offer it thee   135
for a kindness — but cannot you divine what other things of more
value I have about me, that I would more willingly part with?

HELLENA.

Indeed no, that's the business of a witch, and I am but a gypsy
yet. Yet without looking in your hand, I have a parlous guess 'tis
some foolish heart you mean, an inconstant English heart, as lit-   140
tle worth stealing as your purse.

WILLMORE.

Nay, then thou dost deal with the devil, that's certain — thou hast
guessed as right as if thou had'st been one of that number it has

---

124 cross their hands] with silver; payment for telling a fortune

languished for. I find you'll be better acquainted with it, nor can
you take it in a better time; for I am come from the sea, child, 145
and Venus not being propitious to me in her own element, I
have a world of love in store — would you would be good-natured
and take some on't off my hands.

HELLENA.

Why — I could be inclined that way — but for a foolish vow I am
going to make — to die a maid. 150

WILLMORE.

Then thou art damned without redemption, and as I am a good
Christian, I ought in charity to divert so wicked a design — there-
fore prithee, dear creature, let me know quickly when and where
I shall begin to set a helping hand to so good a work.

HELLENA.

If you should prevail with my tender heart (as I begin to fear you 155
will, for you have horrible loving eyes) there will be difficulty in't,
that you'll hardly undergo for my sake.

WILLMORE.

Faith child, I have been bred in dangers, and wear a sword that
has been employed in a worse cause than for a handsome kind
woman — name the danger — let it be anything but a long siege — 160
and I'll undertake it.

HELLENA.

Can you storm?

WILLMORE.

Oh most furiously.

HELLENA.

What think you of a nunnery wall? For he that wins me must gain
that first. 165

WILLMORE.

A nun! Oh how I love thee for't! There's no sinner like a young
saint — nay, now there's no denying me, the old law had no curse
(to a woman) like dying a maid; witness Jepthah's daughter.

---

146 Venus...element] Venus, goddess of love, emerged from the sea.
167 old law] Old Testament law
168 Jephthah's daughter] Jephthah delayed the sacrifice of his virginal daughter for two
    months while she "bewailed her virginity"; see Judges 11: 30-40.

HELLENA.

A very good text this, if well handled, and I perceive, Father Captain, you would impose no severe penance on her who were inclined to console herself, before she took orders.

WILLMORE.

If she be young and handsome.

HELLENA.

Ay, there's it — but if she be not —

WILLMORE.

By this hand, child, I have an implicit faith, and dare venture on thee with all faults — besides, 'tis more meritorious to leave the world when thou hast tasted and proved the pleasure on't. Then, 'twill be a virtue in thee, which now will be pure ignorance.

HELLENA.

I perceive, good Father Captain, you design only to make me fit for heaven — but if on the contrary, you should quite divert me from it and bring me back to the world again, I should have a new man to seek, I find; and what a grief that will be — for when I begin, I fancy I shall love like anything. I never tried yet.

WILLMORE.

Egad and that's kind — prithee dear creature, give me credit for a heart, for faith I'm a very honest fellow. Oh, I long to come first to the banquet of love! And such a swinging appetite I bring — oh, I'm impatient — thy lodging, sweetheart, thy lodging, or I'm a dead man!

HELLENA.

Why must we be either guilty of fornication or murder if we converse with you men — and is there no difference between leave to love me, and leave to lie with me?

WILLMORE.

Faith, child, they were made to go together.

LUCETTA.

Are you sure this is the man?

Pointing to Blunt.

---

171 to take orders] to take religious vows
185 swinging] forcible, immense; also "swingeing"

SANCHO.

    When did I mistake your game?

LUCETTA.

    This is a stranger, I know by his gazing; if he be brisk, he'll ven-
ture to follow me, and then, if I understand my trade, he's mine.   195
He's English too, and they say that's a sort of good-natured loving people, and have generally so kind an opinion of themselves,
that a woman of any wit may flatter 'em into any sort of fool she
pleases.

        She often passes by Blunt and gazes on him;
        he struts and cocks, and walks and gazes on her.

BLUNT.

    'Tis so — she is taken — I have beauties which my false glass at   200
home did not discover.

FLORINDA.

    This woman watches me so, I shall get no opportunity to discover
myself to him, and so miss the intent of my coming — but as I
was saying, sir — [*Looking in his hand*] by this line you should be a
lover.   205

BELVILE.

    I thought how right you guessed,[†] all men are in love, or pretend
to be so — come and let me go, I'm weary of this fooling.

        Walks away.

FLORINDA.

    I will not, till you have confessed whether the passion that you
have vowed Florinda be true or false.

    She holds him, he strives to get from her. He turns quick towards her.

BELVILE.

    Florinda!   210

FLORINDA.

    Softly.

---

200 glass] mirror

BELVILE.

Thou hast named one will fix me here for ever.

FLORINDA.

She'll be disappointed then, who expects you this night at the garden gate, and if you fail not, as — let me see the other hand — you will go near to do — she vows to die or make you happy.   215

Looks on Callis, who observes 'em.

BELVILE.

What canst thou mean?

FLORINDA.

That which I say — farewell.

Offers to go.

BELVILE.

Oh charming sybil, stay, complete that joy which as it is will turn into distraction! Where must I be? At the garden gate? I know it — at night you say? I'll sooner forfeit heaven than disobey.   220

Enter Don Pedro and other masquers, and pass over the stage.

CALLIS.

Madam, your brother's here.

FLORINDA.

Take this to instruct you farther.

Gives him a letter, and goes off.

FREDERICK.

Have a care, sir, what you promise; this may be a trap laid by her brother to ruin you.

BELVILE.

Do not disturb my happiness with doubts.   225

Opens the letter.

---

218 sybil] in Greek antiquity, one who can foretell the future

WILLMORE.

My dear pretty creature, a thousand blessings on thee! Still in this
habit you say? And after dinner at this place?

HELLENA.

Yes, if you will swear to keep your heart, and not bestow it between this and that.

WILLMORE.

By all the little gods of love, I swear I'll leave it with you, and if   230
you run away with it, those deities of justice will revenge me.

Exeunt all the women.

FREDERICK.

Do you know the hand?

BELVILE.

'Tis Florinda's.

All blessings fall upon the virtuous maid.

FREDERICK.

Nay, no idolatry; a sober sacrifice I'll allow you.   235

BELVILE.

Oh friends, the welcomest news! The softest letter! Nay, you shall
all see it! And could you now be serious, I might be made the
happiest man the sun shines on!

WILLMORE.

The reason of this mighty joy?

BELVILE.

See how kindly she invites me to deliver her from the threatened   240
violence of her brother — will you not assist me?

WILLMORE.

I know not what thou mean'st, but I'll make one at any mischief
where a woman's concerned — but she'll be grateful to us for the
favour, will she not?

BELVILE.

How mean you?   245

WILLMORE.

How should I mean? Thou know'st there's but one way for a
woman to oblige me.

BELVILE.

Do not profane — the maid is nicely virtuous.

WILLMORE.

Who, pox, then she's fit for nothing but a husband, let her e'en
go, colonel.   250

FREDERICK.

Peace, she's the colonel's mistress, sir.

WILLMORE.

Let her be the devil; if she be thy mistress, I'll serve her — name
the way.

BELVILE.

Read here this postscript.

Gives him a letter.

WILLMORE.   [*Reads.*]

✳ "At ten at night — at the garden gate — of which, if I cannot get   255
the key, I will contrive a way over the wall — come attended with
a friend or two."
Kind heart, if we three cannot weave a string to let her down a
garden wall, 'twere pity but the hangman wove one for us all.

FREDERICK.

Let her alone for that. Your woman's wit, your fair kind woman,   260
will out-trick a broker or a Jew, and contrive like a Jesuit in
chains — but see, Ned Blunt is stolen out after the lure of a damsel.

Exeunt Blunt and Lucetta.

BELVILE.

So he'll scarce find his way home again, unless we get him cried
by the bellman in the market-place, and 'twould sound prettily —   265
a lost English boy of thirty.

FREDERICK.

I hope 'tis some common crafty sinner, one that will fit him; it
may be she'll sell him for Peru; the rogue's sturdy and would
work well in a mine; at least I hope she'll dress him for our

---

265 bellman] town crier
267 fit] serve him right; punish him fitly
268 Peru] known for its many mines using slave labour

mirth, cheat him of all, then have him well-favouredly hanged   270
and turned out naked at midnight.

WILLMORE.

Prithee, what humour is he of that you wish him so well?

BELVILE.

↑ Why of an English elder brother's humour, educated in a nurs-
ery, with a maid to tend him till fifteen, and lies with his grand-
mother till he's of age; one that knows no pleasure beyond riding   275
to the next fair, or going up to London with his right worshipful
father in Parliament-time, wearing gay clothes, or making honourable love to his lady mother's laundry-maid; gets drunk at a
hunting-match, and ten to one then gives some proofs of his
prowess. A pox upon him, he's our banker and has all our cash   280
about him; and if he fail, we are all broke.

talks about Blunt.

FREDERICK.

Oh let him alone for that matter, he's of a damned stingy quality;
that will secure our stock. I know not in what danger it were indeed if the jilt should pretend she's in love with him, for 'tis a
kind believing coxcomb; otherwise if he part with more than a   285
piece of eight — geld† him; for which offer he may chance to be
beaten, if she be a whore of the first rank.

BELVILE.

Nay, the rogue will not be easily beaten, he's stout enough. Perhaps if they talk beyond his capacity he may chance to exercise
his courage upon some of them, else I'm sure they'll find it as dif-   290
ficult to beat as to please him.

WILLMORE.

'Tis a lucky devil to light upon so kind a wench!

FREDERICK.

Thou had'st a great deal of talk with thy little gypsy; could'st thou
do no good upon her? For mine was hard-hearted.

WILLMORE.

Hang her, she was some damned honest person of quality, I'm   295
sure, she was so very free and witty. If her face be but answerable
to her wit and humour, I would be bound to constancy this
month to gain her — in the meantime, have you made no kind ac-

---

286 geld] castrate; with a play on gold(?)

quaintance since you came to town? You do not use to be honest
so long, gentlemen.   300

FREDERICK.

Faith, love has kept us honest; we have been all fired with a
beauty newly come to town, the famous Paduana, Angellica Bianca.

WILLMORE.

What, the mistress of the dead Spanish general?

BELVILE.

Yes, she's now the only adored beauty of all the youth in Naples,   305
who put on all their charms to appear lovely in her sight, their
coaches, liveries, and themselves, all gay as on a monarch's birth-
day, to attract the eyes of this fair charmer, while she has the
pleasure to behold all languish for her that see her.

FREDERICK.

'Tis pretty to see with how much love the men regard her, and   310
how much envy the women.

WILLMORE.

What gallant has she?

BELVILE.

None, she's exposed to sale,[†] and four days in the week she's
yours — for so much a month.

WILLMORE.

The very thought of it quenches all manner of fire in me — yet   315
prithee let's see her.

BELVILE.

Let's first to dinner, and after that we'll pass the day as you
please — but at night ye must all be at my devotion.

WILLMORE.

I will not fail you.

---

302 Paduana] a woman from Padua

ACT II
Scene I. The Long Street

*Enter Belvile and Frederick in masquing habits, and Willmore in his own
clothes, with a vizard in his hand.*

WILLMORE.
But why thus disguised and muzzled?
BELVILE.
Because whatever extravagances we commit in these faces, our
own may not be obliged to answer 'em.
WILLMORE.
I should have changed my eternal buff too; but no matter, my lit-
tle gipsy would not have found me out then, for if she should   5
change hers, it is impossible I should know her, unless I should
hear her prattle. A pox on't, I cannot get her out of my head;
pray heaven, if ever I do see her again, she prove damnably ugly,
that I may fortify myself against her tongue.
BELVILE.
Have a care of love, for o'my conscience she was not of a quality   10
to give thee any hopes.
WILLMORE.
Pox on 'em, why do they draw a man in then? She has played
with my heart so, that 'twill never lie still till I have met with some
kind wench that will play the game out with me — oh, for my
arms full of soft, white, kind — woman — such as I fancy Angel-   15
lica.
BELVILE.
This is her house, if you were but in stock to get admittance.
They have not dined yet; I perceive the picture is not out.

Enter Blunt.

WILLMORE.
I long to see the shadow of the fair substance; a man may gaze on
that for nothing.   20

Stage Direction: vizard] mask
4 buff] hard-wearing dull yellow leather used in soldiers' coats

BLUNT.

Colonel, thy hand — and thine, Fred. I have been an ass, a de-
luded fool, a very coxcomb from my birth till this hour, and
heartily repent my little faith.

BELVILE.

What the devil's the matter with thee, Ned?

BLUNT.[†]

Oh such a mistress[†] Fred, such a girl!   25

WILLMORE.

Ha! where?

FREDERICK.[†]

Ay, where!

BLUNT.[†]

So fond, so amorous, so toying and so fine! And all for sheer
love, ye rogue! Oh how she looked and kissed! And soothed my
heart from my bosom — I cannot think I was awake, and yet me-   30
thinks I see and feel her charms still — Fred, try if she have not
left the taste of her balmy kisses upon my lips.

Kisses him.

BELVILE.

Ha! Ha! Ha!

WILLMORE.[†]

Death, man, where is she?

BLUNT.[†]

What a dog was I to stay in dull England so long. How have I   35
laughed at the colonel when he sighed for love! But now the little
archer has revenged him! And by this one dart, I can guess at all
his joys, which then I took for fancies, mere dreams and fables.
Well, I'm resolved to sell all in Essex, and plant here for ever.

BELVILE.

What a blessing 'tis thou hast a mistress thou dar'st boast of, for I   40
know thy humour is rather to have a proclaimed clap than a secret amour.

---

36 little archer] Cupid
41 clap] venereal disease

WILLMORE.

Dost know her name?

BLUNT.

Her name? No, 'sheartlikins, what care I for names? She's fair!
Young! Brisk and kind, even to ravishment! And what a pox care   45
I for knowing her by any other title?

WILLMORE.

Didst give her anything?

BLUNT.

Give her! Ha, ha, ha! Why she's a person of quality — that's a
good one, give her! 'Sheartlikins, dost think such creatures are to
be bought? Or are we provided for such a purchase? Give her,   50
quoth ye? Why, she presented me with this bracelet for the toy of
a diamond I used to wear. No, gentlemen, Ned Blunt is not everybody. She expects me again tonight.

WILLMORE.

Egad, that's well; we'll all go.

BLUNT.

Not a soul. No, gentlemen, you are wits; I am a dull country   55
rogue, I.

FREDERICK.

Well, sir, for all your person of quality, I shall be very glad to understand your purse be secure; 'tis our whole estate at present,
which we are loath to hazard in one bottom; come, sir, unlade.

BLUNT.

Take the necessary trifle useless now to me, that am beloved by   60
such a gentlewoman — 'sheartlikins, money! Here, take mine too.

FREDERICK.

No, keep that to be cozened, that we may laugh.

WILLMORE.

Cozened — death! Would I could meet with one that would cozen
me of all the love I could spare tonight.

FREDERICK.

Pox, 'tis some common whore, upon my life.   65

---

59 bottom] keel or hull of a ship; a cargo ship
62 cozened] cheated

BLUNT.

A whore! Yes, with such clothes! Such jewels! Such a house! Such furniture, and so attended! A whore!

BELVILE.

Why yes, sir, they are whores, though they'll neither entertain you with drinking, swearing, or bawdry; are whores in all those gay clothes and right jewels; are whores with those great houses richly furnished with velvet beds, store of plate, handsome attendance and fine coaches; are whores, and errant ones.

WILLMORE.

Pox on't, where do these fine whores live?

BELVILE.

Where no rogues in office ycleped constables dare give 'em laws, nor the wine-inspired bullies of the town break their windows; yet they are whores, though this Essex calf believe 'em persons of quality.

BLUNT.

'Sheartlikins, y'are all fools; there are things about this Essex calf that shall take with the ladies, beyond all your wit and parts – this shape and size, gentlemen, are not to be despised – my waist,† too, tolerably long, with other inviting signs, that shall be nameless.

WILLMORE.

Egad, I believe he may have met with some person of quality that may be kind to him.

BELVILE.

Dost thou perceive any such tempting things about him, that should make a fine woman, and of quality, pick him out from all mankind to throw away her youth and beauty upon, nay and her dear heart too! No, no, Angellica has raised the price too high.

WILLMORE.

May she languish for mankind till she die, and be damned for that one sin alone.

71 plate] silver-plated items
74 ycleped] called, named
76 Essex calf] fool; a native of Essex. Blunt's home county of Essex was famous for its calves.

Enter two bravoes, and hang up a great picture of Angellica's against the balcony, and two little ones at each side of the door.

BELVILE.

See there, the fair sign to the inn where a man may lodge that's fool enough to give her price.

Willmore gazes on the picture.

BLUNT.

'Sheartlikins, gentlemen, what's this!

BELVILE.

A famous courtesan, that's to be sold.

BLUNT.

How? To be sold! Nay then, I have nothing to say to her — sold!   95
What impudence is practiced in this country? With what order
and decency whoring's established here by virtue of the Inquisition. Come, let's begone, I'm sure we're no chapmen for this
commodity.

FREDERICK.

Thou art none, I'm sure, unless thou could'st have her in thy bed   100
at a price of a coach in the street.

WILLMORE.

How wondrous fair she is. A thousand crowns a month — by
heaven, as many kingdoms were too little; a plague of this poverty — of which I ne'er complain but when it hinders my approach to beauty which virtue ne'er could purchase.   105

Turns from the picture.

BLUNT.

What's this? [*Reads.*]
A thousand crowns a month!
'Sheartlikins, here's a sum! Sure 'tis a mistake.
— Hark you friend, does she take or give so much by the month?

110

---

102 crown] gold coin, value 5 shillings

…

FREDERICK.
  A thousand crowns! Why 'tis a portion for the Infanta.
BLUNT.
  Harkee, friends, won't she trust?
BRAVO.
  This is a trade, sir, that cannot live by credit.

Enter Don Pedro in masquerade, followed by Stephano.

BELVILE.
  See, here's more company; let's walk off a while.

Exeunt English. Pedro reads.

Enter Angellica and Moretta in the balcony, and draw a silk curtain.

PEDRO.
  Fetch me a thousand crowns, I never wished to buy this beauty at
  an easier rate.   115

Passes off.

ANGELLICA.
  Prithee what said those fellows to thee?
BRAVO.
  Madam, the first were admirers of beauty only, but no purchas-
  ers; they were merry with your price and picture, laughed at the
  sum, and so passed off.
ANGELLICA.
  No matter, I'm not displeased with their rallying; their wonder   120
  feeds my vanity, and he that wishes but to buy gives me more
  pride than he that gives my price can make my pleasure.
BRAVO.
  Madam, the last I knew through all his disguises to be Don Pe-
  dro, nephew to the general, and who was with him in Pamplona.

---

110 Infanta] daughter of the Spanish king
111 harkee] hark ye, listen

Prostitute : she makes chooses for who she wants.

ANGELLICA.

Don Pedro! My old gallant's nephew. When his uncle died he left   125
him a vast sum of money; it is he who was so in love with me at
Padua, and who used to make the general so jealous.

MORETTA.

Is this he that used to prance before our window, and take such
care to show himself an amorous ass? If I am not mistaken, he is
the likeliest man to give your price.   130

ANGELLICA.

The man is brave and generous, but of an humour so uneasy and
inconstant, that the victory over his heart is as soon lost as won, a
slave that can add little to the triumph of the conqueror. But inconstancy's the sin of all mankind; therefore I'm resolved that
nothing but gold shall charm my heart.   135

MORETTA.

I'm glad on't; 'tis only interest that women of our profession
ought to consider, though I wonder what has kept you from that
general disease of our sex so long, I mean that of being in love.

ANGELLICA.

A kind but sullen star under which I had the happiness to be
born. Yet I have had no time for love; the bravest and noblest of   140
mankind have purchased my favours at so dear a rate as if no
coin but gold were current with our trade – but here's Don Pedro again, fetch me my lute – for 'tis for him or Don Antonio the
viceroy's son, that I have spread my nets.

*Enter at one door Don Pedro, Stephano; Don Antonio and Diego (Page)‡ at
the other door, with people following him in masquerade, anticly attired,
some with music; they both go up to the picture.*

ANTONIO.

A thousand crowns! Had not the painter flattered her, I should   145
not think it dear.

PEDRO.

Flattered her! By heav'n, he cannot; I have seen the original, nor
is there one charm here more than adorns her face and eyes; all

---

125 gallant] fine gentleman; lover or paramour
146 dear] expensive
‡ stage direction added by editor

this soft and sweet, with a certain languishing air, that no artist
can represent. 150

ANTONIO.

What I heard of her beauty before had fired my soul, but this
confirmation of it has blown it to a flame.

PEDRO.

Ha!

PAGE.

Sir, I have known you throw away a thousand crowns on a worse
face, and though y'are near your marriage, you may venture a lit- 155
tle love here. Florinda will not miss it.

PEDRO. [*Aside.*]

Ha! Florinda! Sure 'tis Antonio.

ANTONIO.

Florinda! Name not those distant joys; there's not one thought of
her will check my passion here.

PEDRO.

Florinda scorned! And all my hopes defeated of the possession of
Angellica. 160

A noise of a lute above. Antonio gazes up.

Her injuries, by heaven, he shall not boast of.

Song to a lute above.

SONG.

When Damon first began to love
He languished in a soft desire,
And knew not how the gods to move, 165
To lessen or increase his fire.
For Caelia in her charming eyes
Wore all love's sweets, and all his cruelties.
II.
But as beneath a shade he lay,
Weaving of flow'rs for Caelia's hair, 170
She chanced to lead her flock that way,
And saw the am'rous shepherd there.
She gazed around upon the place,
And saw the grove (resembling night)
To all the joys of love invite, 175

Whilst guilty smiles and blushes dressed her face.
At this the bashful youth all transport grew,
And with kind force he taught the virgin how
To yield what all his sighs could never do.

*Angellica throws open the curtains and bows to Antonio, who pulls off his
vizard and bows and blows up kisses.*

Pedro unseen looks in's face.

ANTONIO.
By Heav'n she's charming fair!   180
PEDRO.
'Tis he; the false Antonio!
ANTONIO.   [*To the bravo.*]
Friend, where must I pay my offering of love?
My thousand crowns I mean.
PEDRO.
That offering I have designed to make.
And yours will come too late.   185
ANTONIO.
Prithee begone, I shall grow angry else.
And then thou art not safe.
PEDRO.
My anger may be fatal, sir, as yours,
And he that enters here may prove this truth.
ANTONIO.
I know not who thou art, but I am sure thou'rt worth my killing,   190
for aiming at Angellica.

They draw and fight. Enter Willmore and Blunt who draw and part 'em.

BLUNT.
'Sheartlikins, here's fine doings.
WILLMORE.
Tilting for the wench, I'm sure — nay, gad, if that would win her,
I have as good a sword as the best of ye. Put up — put up, and
take another time and place, for this is designed for lovers only.   195

They all put up.

PEDRO.

    We are prevented; dare you meet me tomorrow on the Molo?

    For I've a title to a better quarrel,

    That of Florinda, in whose credulous heart

    Thou'st made an int'rest and destroyed my hopes.

ANTONIO.

    Dare!   200

    I'll meet thee there as early as the day.

PEDRO.

    We will come thus disguised that whosoever chance to get the

    better, he may escape unknown.

ANTONIO.

    It shall be so.

Exeunt Pedro and Stephano.

    Who should this rival be? Unless the English colonel, of whom   205

    I've often heard Don Pedro speak; it must be he, and time he

    were removed, who lays claim to all my happiness.

Willmore having gazed all this while on the picture, pulls down a little one.

WILLMORE.

    This posture's loose and negligent,

    The sight on't would beget a warm desire

    In souls whom impotence and age had chilled.   210

    This must along with me.

BRAVO.

    What means this rudeness, sir? Restore the picture.

ANTONIO.

    Ha! Rudeness committed to the fair Angellica! Restore the pic-

    ture, sir —

WILLMORE.

    Indeed I will not, sir.   215

ANTONIO.

    By heaven, but you shall.

---

193 tilting for] fighting for; charging on horseback against an opponent with a lance
196 the Molo] pier; from "môle" (Fr.).

WILLMORE.

    Nay, do not show your sword; if you do, by this dear beauty — I will show mine too.

ANTONIO.

    What right can you pretend to't?

WILLMORE.

    That of possession, which I will maintain — you perhaps have a thousand[†] crowns to give for the original.   220

ANTONIO.

    No matter, sir, you shall restore the picture.

Angellica and Moretta above.

ANGELLICA.

    Oh Moretta! What's the matter?

ANTONIO.

    Or leave your life behind.   225

WILLMORE.

    Death! you lie — I will do neither.

They fight; the Spaniards join with Antonio; Blunt laying on like mad.

ANGELLICA.

    Hold, I command you, if for me you fight.[†]

They leave off and bow.

WILLMORE.

    How heavenly fair she is! Ah, plague of her price.

ANGELLICA.

    You sir, in buff, you that appear a soldier, that first began this in- solence —

WILLMORE.

    'Tis true, I did so, if you call it insolence for a man to preserve   230 himself. I saw your charming picture and was wounded; quite through my soul each pointed beauty ran, and, wanting a thou- sand crowns to procure my remedy, I laid this little picture to my bosom — which if you cannot allow me, I'll resign.

ANGELLICA.

    No, you may keep the trifle.   235

ANTONIO.

    You shall first ask me leave, and this.

Fight again as before.

Enter Belvile and Frederick who join with the English.

ANGELLICA.

Hold! Will you ruin me? Biskey — Sebastian — part 'em.

The Spaniards are beaten off.

MORETTA.

Oh madam, we're undone. A pox upon that rude fellow, he's set
on to ruin us; we shall never see good days till all these fighting
poor rogues are sent to the galleys.   240

Enter Belvile, Blunt, Frederick, and Willmore with's shirt bloody.

BLUNT.

'Sheartlikins, beat me at this sport, and I'll ne'er wear sword
more.

BELVILE.

The devil's in thee for a mad fellow; thou art always one at an unlucky adventure — come, let's begone whilst we're safe, and remember these are Spaniards, a sort of people that know how to   245
revenge an affront.

FREDERICK.   [*To Willmore.*]

You bleed! I hope you are not wounded.

WILLMORE.

Not much — a plague on your dons; if they fight no better they'll
ne'er recover Flanders. What the devil was't to them that I took
down the picture?   250

BLUNT.

Took it! 'Sheartlikins, we'll have the great one too; 'tis ours by
conquest. Prithee help me up and I'll pull it down —

ANGELLICA.

Stay sir, and ere you affront me farther, let me know how you
durst commit this outrage — to you I speak, sir, for you appear a
gentleman.   255

WILLMORE.

To me, madam — gentlemen, your servant.

Belvile stays him.

BELVILE.

Is the devil in thee? Dost know the danger of entering the house
of an incensed courtesan?

WILLMORE.

I thank you for your care — but there are other matters in hand, there are, though we have no great temptation. Death! Let me   260
go.

FREDERICK.

Yes, to your lodging if you will, but not in here. Damn these gay harlots — by this hand I'll have as sound and handsome a whore for a patacoon — death, man, she'll murder thee.

WILLMORE.

Oh! Fear me not, shall I not venture where a beauty calls? A   265
lovely charming beauty! For fear of danger! When by Heaven there's none so great as to long for her whilst I want money† to purchase her.

FREDERICK.†

Therefore 'tis loss of time unless you had the thousand crowns to pay.   270

WILLMORE.

It may be she may give a favour; at least I shall have the pleasure of saluting her when I enter, and when I depart.

BELVILE.

Pox, she'll as soon lie with thee as kiss thee, and sooner stab than do either — you shall not go.

ANGELLICA.

Fear not sir, all I have to wound with is my eyes.   275

BLUNT.

Let him go. 'Sheartlikins, I believe the gentlewoman means well.

BELVILE.

Well, take thy fortune; we'll expect you in the next street — fare-well, fool — farewell —

WILLMORE.

Bye† colonel —

Goes in.

FREDERICK.

The rogue's stark mad for a wench.

Exeunt.   280

---

264 patacoon] Spanish coin; value in seventeenth century, 4s.8d.

Scene II. A fine Chamber.

Enter Willmore, Angellica and Moretta.

ANGELLICA.

Insolent sir, how durst you pull down my picture?

WILLMORE.

Rather, how durst you set it up, to tempt poor amorous mortals
with so much excellence, which I find you have but too well consulted by the unmerciful price you set upon't. Is all this heaven of
beauty shown to move despair in those that cannot buy? And can   5
you think th'effects of that despair should be less extravagant
than I have shown?

ANGELLICA.

I sent for you to ask my pardon sir, not to aggravate your crime
— I thought I should have seen you at my feet imploring it.

WILLMORE.

You are deceived; I came to rail at you, and rail such truths too,   10
as shall let you see the vanity of that pride which taught you how
to set such price on sin. For such it is, whilst that which is love's
due is meanly bartered for.

ANGELLICA.

Ha! ha! ha! Alas, good captain, what pity 'tis your edifying doc-
trine will do no good upon me — Moretta! Fetch the gentleman a   15
glass, and let him survey himself, to see what charms he has —
[*Aside in a soft tone*] and guess my business.

MORETTA.

He knows himself of old; I believe those breeches and he have
been acquainted ever since he was beaten at Worcester.

ANGELLICA.

Nay, do not abuse the poor creature —   20

19 Worcester] The Battle of Worcester (1651) was the final defeat of Prince Charles by
the Parliamentary forces, after which he fled to the continent.

MORETTA.

> Good weather-beaten corporal, will you march off? We have no need of your doctrine, though you have of our charity, but at present we have no scraps, we can afford no kindness for God's sake; in fine, sirrah, the price is too high i'th'mouth for you, therefore troop, I say. 25

WILLMORE.

> Here, good forewoman of the shop, serve me, and I'll be gone.

MORETTA.

> Keep it to pay your laundress, your linen stinks of the gunroom; for here's no selling by retail.

WILLMORE.

> Thou hast sold plenty of thy stale ware at a cheap rate.

MORETTA.

> Ay, the more silly kind heart I, but this is an age wherein beauty 30 is at higher rates. In fine, you know the price of this.

WILLMORE.

> I grant you 'tis here — set down a thousand crowns a month — pray, how much may come to my share for a pistole? Bawd, take your black lead and sum it up, that I may have a pistole's†worth of this vain gay thing,† and I'll trouble you no more. 35

MORETTA.

> Pox on him, he'll fret me to death — abominable fellow, I tell thee, we only sell by the whole piece.

WILLMORE.

> 'Tis very hard, the whole cargo or nothing. Faith, madam, my stock will not reach it; I cannot be your chapman — yet I have countrymen in town, merchants of love like me; I'll see if they'll 40 put in for a share. We cannot lose much by it, and what we have no use for, we'll sell upon the Friday's mart at "Who gives more?" I am studying, madam, how to purchase you, though at present I am unprovided of money.

ANGELLICA. [*Aside*]‡

> Sure, this from any other man would anger me — nor shall he know the conquest he has made

---

24 high i'th'mouth] above one's rank; elevated
33 pistole]gold coin; value between 16s.6d. and 18s .
34 black lead] pencil

trying to convince Angelica ←

— Poor angry man, how I despise this railing.

WILLMORE.

Yes, I am poor — but I am a gentleman,
And one that scorns this baseness which you practice;
Poor as I am, I would not sell myself,   50
No, not to gain your charming high prized person.
Though I admire you strangely for your beauty,
Yet I contemn your mind.
And yet I would at any rate enjoy you
At your own rate — but cannot. See here   55
The only sum I can command on earth;
I know not where to eat when this is gone.
Yet such a slave I am to love and beauty
This last reserve I'll sacrifice to enjoy you.
Nay, do not frown, I know you're to be bought,   60
And would be bought by me, by me,
For a mean trifling sum if I could pay it down;
Which happy knowledge I will still repeat,
And lay it to my heart; it has a virtue in't,
And soon will cure those wounds your eyes have made.   65
And yet — there's something so divinely powerful there —
Nay, I will gaze — to let you see my strength.

Holds her, looks on her, and pauses and sighs.

By heav'n, bright creature — I would not for the world
Thy fame were half so fair as is thy face.

Turns her away from him.

ANGELICA. [*Aside.*] ← *completely smitten.*
His words go through me to the very soul.   70
— If you have nothing else to say to me —

WILLMORE.

Yes, you shall hear how infamous you are —
For which I do not hate thee —
But that secures my heart, and all the flames it feels

---

53 contemn] have contempt for

Are but so many lusts —   75
I know it by their sudden bold intrusion.
The fire's impatient and betrays, 'tis false —
For had it been the purer flame of love,
I should have pined and languished at your feet,
Ere found the impudence to have discovered it.   80
I now dare stand your scorn, and your denial.

MORETTA.

Sure she's bewitched,[†] that she can stand thus tamely and hear
his saucy railing — sirrah, will you be gone?

ANGELLICA. [*To Moretta.*]

How dare you take this liberty? Withdraw.
—Pray tell me, sir, are not you guilty of the same mercenary crime?   85
When a lady is proposed to you for a wife, you never ask how
fair, discreet, or virtuous she is, but what's her fortune — which if
but small, you cry, "She will not do my business" and basely leave
her, though[†] she languish for you — say, is not this as poor?

WILLMORE.

It is a barbarous custom, which I will scorn to defend in our sex,   90
and do despise in yours.

ANGELLICA.

Thou'rt a brave fellow! Put up thy gold, and know,
That were thy fortune as large as thy soul,
Thou should'st not buy my love,
Couldst thou forget those mean effects of vanity   95
Which set me out to sale, and, as a lover, prize my yielding joys.
Canst thou believe they'll be entirely thine,
Without considering they were mercenary?

WILLMORE.

I cannot tell, I must bethink me first. [*Aside.*] — Ha — death, I'm
going to believe her.   100

ANGELLICA.

Prithee confirm that faith — or if thou canst not — flatter me a little, 'twill please me from thy mouth.

WILLMORE. [*Aside.*]

Curse on thy charming tongue! Dost thou return
My feigned contempt with so much subtlety?

---

92 put up] put away

— Thou'st found the easiest way into my heart,   105
Though I yet know that all thou say'st is false.

Turning from her in rage.

ANGELLICA.
By all that's good, 'tis real;
I never loved before, though oft a mistress.
Shall my first vows be slighted?
WILLMORE.   [*Aside.*]
What can she mean?   110
ANGELLICA.   [*In an angry tone.*]
I find you cannot credit me.
WILLMORE.
I know you take me for an errant ass,
An ass that may be soothed into belief
And then be used at pleasure;
But madam, I have been so often cheated   115
By perjured soft deluding hypocrites,
That I've no faith left for the cozening sex;
Especially for women of your trade.
ANGELLICA.
The low esteem you have of me, perhaps
May bring my heart again: 120
For I have pride, that yet surmounts my love.

She turns with pride; he holds her.

WILLMORE.
Throw off this pride, this enemy to bliss,
And show the pow'r of love; 'tis with those arms
I can be only vanquished, made a slave.
ANGELLICA.
Is all my mighty expectation vanished?   125
No, I will not hear thee talk — thou hast a charm
In every word that draws my heart away.
And all the thousand trophies I designed
Thou hast undone — why art thou soft?
Thy looks are bravely rough, and meant for war.   130
Could'st thou not storm on still?
I then perhaps had been as free as thou.

WILLMORE.   [*Aside.*]

　　Death, how she throws her fire about my soul!
　　— Take heed, fair creature, how you raise my hopes,
　　Which once assumed pretends to all dominion.　　　　　　135
　　There's not a joy thou hast in store,
　　I shall not then command.
　　For which I'll pay thee back my soul, my life!
　　Come, let's begin th'account this happy minute!

ANGELLICA.

　　And will you pay me then the price I ask?　　　　　　140

WILLMORE.

　　Oh, why dost thou draw me from an awful worship,
　　By showing thou art no divinity?
　　Conceal the fiend, and show me the angel!
　　Keep me but ignorant, and I'll be devout
　　And pay my vows for ever at this shrine.　　*Swears*　　　145
　　　　　　　　　　　　　　　　　　　　　　　constincy.

　　　　　　Kneels and kisses her hand.

ANGELLICA.

　　The pay I mean, is but thy love for mine.
　　Can you give that?

WILLMORE.

　　Entirely — come, let's withdraw! Where I'll renew my vows — and
　　breathe 'em with such ardour thou shalt not doubt my zeal.

ANGELLICA.

　　Thou hast a pow'r too strong to be resisted.　　　　　　150

　　　　　　Exeunt Willmore and Angellica.

MORETTA.　—> *says Wil is an enemy to*
　　　　　　　　　　their trade.
　　Now my curse go with you — is all our project fallen to this? To
　　love the only enemy to our trade? Nay, to love such a shameroon,
　　a very beggar, nay a pirate beggar, whose business is to rifle, and

---

153 shameroon] one who deceives or uses false pretenses

be gone, a no-purchase, no-pay tatterdemalion and English
picaroon. A rogue that fights for daily drink, and takes a pride in   155
being loyally lousy — oh, I could curse now, if I durst. This is the
fate of most whores.
Trophies, which from believing fops we win,
Are spoils to those who cozen us again.

---

154 tatterdemalion] a person with tattered clothes
155 picaroon] rogue, pirate
156 lousy] to have lice

ACT III.
Scene I. A Street.

Enter Florinda, Valeria, Hellena, in antic different dresses from what they were in before. Callis attending.

Teasing Hellena.

FLORINDA.

I wonder what should make my brother in so ill a humour? I hope he has not found out our ramble this morning.

HELLENA.

No, if he had, we should have heard on't at both ears, and have been mewed up this afternoon; which I would not for the world should have happened — hey ho, I'm as sad as a lover's lute.   5

VALERIA.

Well, methinks we have learnt this trade of gypsies as readily as if we have been bred upon the road to Loreto;† and yet I did so fumble when I told the stranger his fortune, that I was afraid I should have told my own and yours by mistake — but methinks Hellena has been very serious ever since.   10

FLORINDA.

I would give my garters she were in love, to be revenged upon her for abusing me — how is't, Hellena?

HELLENA.

Ah — would I had never seen my mad monsieur — and yet for all your laughing, I am not in love — and yet this small acquaintance, o' my conscience, will never out of my head.   15

VALERIA.

Ha, ha, ha — I laugh to think how thou art fitted with a lover, a fellow that I warrant loves every new face he sees.

HELLENA.

Hum — he has not kept his word with me here — and may be taken up — that thought is not very pleasant to me — what the deuce should this be now, that I feel?   20

VALERIA.

What is't like?

---

4 mewed] caged; from "mew," a cage for hawks
7 Loreto] a city in Italy famous as a place of pilgrimage

HELLENA.

Nay, the lord knows — but if I should be hanged, I cannot choose
but be angry and afraid when I think that mad fellow should be
in love with any body but me — what to think of myself, I know
not — would I could meet with some true damned gypsy, that I 25
might know my fortune.

VALERIA.

Know it! Why there's nothing so easy; thou wilt love this wander-
ing inconstant till thou find'st thyself hanged about his neck, and
then be as mad to get free again.

FLORINDA.

Yes, Valeria, we shall see her bestride his baggage horse, and fol- 30
low him to the campaign.

HELLENA.

So, so, now you are provided for there's no care taken of poor
me — but since you have set my heart a-wishing — I am resolved
to know for what; I will not die of the pip, so I will not.

FLORINDA.

Art thou mad to talk so? Who will like thee well enough to have 35
thee, that hears what a mad wench thou art?

HELLENA.

Like me! I don't intend every he that likes me shall have me, but
he that I like; I should have stayed in the nunnery still, if I had
liked my lady Abbess as well as she liked me — no, I came thence
not (as my wise brother imagines) to take an eternal farewell of
the world, but to love and to be beloved, and I will be beloved, or 40
I'll get one of your men, so I will.

VALERIA.

Am I put into the number of lovers?

HELLENA.

You? Why coz, I know thou'rt too good-natured to leave us in
any design; thou would† venture a cast, though thou comest off a 45
loser, especially with such a gamester. I observe your man, and
your willing ear incline that way; and if you are not a lover, 'tis an
art soon learnt — that I find.

Sighs.

---

34 the pip] depression, ill temper

FLORINDA.

I wonder how you learnt to love so easily; I had a thousand[†]
charms to meet my eyes and ears ere I could yield, and 'twas the   50
knowledge of Belvile's merit, not the surprising person, took my
soul — thou art too rash, to give a heart at first sight.

HELLENA.

Hang your considering lover; I never thought beyond the fancy
that 'twas a very pretty, idle, silly kind of pleasure to pass one's
time with, to write little soft nonsensical billets, and with great   55
difficulty and danger receive answers in which I shall have my
beauty praised, my wit admired, (though little or none) and have
the vanity and power to know I am desirable; then I have the
more inclination that way, because I am to be a nun, and so shall
not be suspected to have any such earthly thoughts about me —   60
but when I walk thus — and sigh thus — they'll think my mind's
upon my monastery, and cry how happy 'tis she's so resolved.
But not a word[†] of man.

FLORINDA.

What a mad creature's this?

HELLENA.

I'll warrant, if my brother hears either of you sigh, he cries   65
(gravely) — I fear you have the indiscretion to be in love, but take
heed of the honour of our house, and your own unspotted fame,
and so he conjures on till he has laid the soft-winged god in your
hearts, or broke the bird's nest — but see, here comes your lover,
but where's my inconstant? Let's step aside, and we may learn   70
something.

Go aside.

Enter Belvile, Frederick and Blunt.

BELVILE.

What means this! The picture's taken in.

BLUNT.

It may be the wench is good-natured, and will be kind gratis.
Your friend's a proper handsome fellow.

---

55 billets] love notes

BELVILE.

    I rather think she has cut his throat and is fled: I am mad he   75
should throw himself into dangers — pox on't, I shall want him
too at night — let's knock and ask for him.

HELLENA.

    My heart goes a-pit a-pat, for fear 'tis my man they talk of.[†]

Knock; Moretta above.

MORETTA.

    What would you have!

BELVILE.

    Tell the stranger that entered here about two hours ago that his   80
friends stay here for him.

MORETTA.

    A curse upon him for Moretta; would he were at the devil — but
he's coming to you.

Enter Willmore.[†]

HELLENA.

    Ay, ay,[†] 'tis he! Oh how this vexes me.

BELVILE.

    And how and how dear lad, has fortune smiled? Are we to break   85
her windows? Or raise up altars to her, hah?

WILLMORE.

    Does not my fortune sit triumphant on my brow? Dost not see
the little wanton god there all gay and smiling? Have I not an air
about my face and eyes that distinguish me from the crowd of
common lovers? By heaven, Cupid's quiver has not half so many   90
darts as her eyes! Oh, such a bona roba! To sleep in her arms is
lying in fresco, all perfumed air about me.

HELLENA.   *[Aside.]*

    Here's fine encouragement for me to fool on.

[Handwritten annotation: Boasting about being in Angelica.]

[Handwritten annotation: Here's some fine lines to play with]

---

91 bona roba] literally, good dress; figuratively, compliant woman, courtesan
92 in fresco] in fresh air, outside

WILLMORE.

Harkee, where didst thou purchase that rich Canary we drank today! Tell me, that I may adore the spigot and sacrifice to the   95
butt! The juice was divine into which I must dip my rosary, and
then bless all things that I would have bold or fortunate.

BELVILE.

Well sir, let's go take a bottle, and hear the story of your success.

FREDERICK.

Would not French wine do better?

WILLMORE.

Damn the hungry balderdash, cheerful sack has a generous vir-   100
tue in't inspiring a successful confidence; gives eloquence to the
tongue, and vigour to the soul, and has in a few hours completed
all my hopes and wishes! There's nothing left to raise a new desire in me — come let's be gay and wanton — and gentlemen,
study, study what you want, for here are friends that will supply   105
gentlemen — hark! What a charming sound they make — 'tis he
and she gold† whilst here, and shall beget new pleasures every
moment.

BLUNT.

But harkee sir, you are not married, are you?

WILLMORE.

✳All the honey of matrimony, but none of the sting, friend.   110

BLUNT.

'Sheartlikins, thou'rt a fortunate rogue!

WILLMORE.

I am so sir, let these — inform you! Ha, how sweetly they chime!
Pox of poverty, it makes a man a slave, makes wit and honour
sneak, my soul grew lean and rusty for want of credit.

BLUNT.

'Sheartlikins, this I like well, it looks like my lucky bargain! Oh   115
how I long for the approach of my squire, that is to conduct me
to her house again. Why — here's two provided for.

---

94 Canary] wine from the Canary Islands; first of a series of metaphors drawn from
    winemaking and drinking
96 butt] cask for wine or ale
100 balderdash] a mixture of alcoholic drinks
100 sack] white wine from Spain and Canary Islands

FREDERICK.
By this light y'are happy men.

BLUNT.
Fortune is pleased to smile on us, gentlemen — to smile on us.

Enter Sancho and pulls down Blunt by the sleeve.

SANCHO.
Sir, my lady expects you —   120

They go aside.

She has remov'd all that might oppose your will and pleasure —
and is impatient till you come.

BLUNT.
Sir, I'll attend you — oh, the happiest rogue! I'll take no leave,
lest[†] they either dog me, or stay me.

Exit with Sancho.

BELVILE.
But then the little gypsy is forgot?   125

WILLMORE.
A mischief on thee for putting her into my thoughts. I had quite
forgot her else, and this night's debauch had drunk her quite
down.

HELLENA.
Had it so, good captain!

Claps him on the back.

WILLMORE. [*Aside.*]
Hah! I hope she did not hear me.   130

HELLENA.
What, afraid of such a champion?

WILLMORE.
Oh! you're a fine lady of your word, are you not? To make a man
languish a whole day —

HELLENA.
In tedious search of me.

WILLMORE.

Egad child, thou'rt in the right; had'st thou seen what a melan-   135
choly dog I have been ever since I was a lover, how I have walked
the streets like a Capuchin with my hands in my sleeves — faith,
sweetheart, thou would'st pity me.

HELLENA.   [*Aside*]‡

Now if I should be hanged I can't be angry with him, he dissem-
bles so heartily   140
— alas, good captain, what pains you have taken — now were I ungrateful not to reward so true a servant.

WILLMORE.

Poor soul! That's kindly said; I see thou barest† a conscience —
come then, for a beginning show me thy dear face.

HELLENA.

I'm afraid, my small acquaintance, you have been staying that   145
swinging stomach you boasted this morning; I then remember
my little collation would have gone down with you, without the
sauce of a handsome face — is your stomach so queasy now?

WILLMORE.

Faith, long fasting, child, spoils a man's appetite — yet if you
durst treat, I could so lay about me still —   150

HELLENA.

And would you fall to, before a priest says grace?

WILLMORE.

Oh fie, fie, what an old, out of fashioned thing hast thou named?
Thou could'st not dash me more out of countenance should'st
thou show me an ugly face.

*Whilst he is seemingly courting Hellena, enter Angellica, Moretta, Biskey
and Sebastian, all in masquerade; Angellica sees Willmore and stares.*

ANGELLICA.

Heavens 'tis† he! And passionately fond to see another woman.   155

MORETTA.

What could you less expect from such a swaggerer?

ANGELLICA.

Expect! As much as I paid him, a heart entire

---

137 Capuchin] a friar of the order of St. Francis
147 collation] light meal

Which I had pride enough to think when ere I gave,
It would have raised the man above the vulgar,
Made him all soul, and that all soft and constant.   160

HELLENA.

You see, captain, how willing I am to be friends with you, till time
and ill luck make us lovers, and ask you the question first, rather
than put your modesty to the blush by asking me (for alas!) I
know you captains are such strict men, and such severe observers
of your vows to chastity, that 'twill be hard to prevail with your   165
tender conscience to marry a young willing maid.

WILLMORE.

Do not abuse me, for fear I should take thee at thy word, and
marry thee indeed, which I'm sure will be revenge sufficient.

HELLENA.

O' my conscience, that will be our destiny, because we are both
of one humour; I am as inconstant as you, for I have considered,   170
captain, that a handsome woman has a great deal to do whilst her
face is good, for then is our harvest-time to gather friends; and
should I in these days of my youth catch a fit of foolish constancy, I were undone; 'tis loitering by daylight in our great jour-
ney. Therefore, I declare I'll allow but one year for love, one year   175
for indifference, and one year for hate — and then — go hang
yourself — for I profess myself the gay, the kind, and the inconstant — the devil's in't if this won't please you.

WILLMORE.

Oh most damnably — I have a heart with a hole quite through it
too; no prison mine to keep a mistress in.   180

ANGELLICA.   [*Aside.*]

Perjured man! How I believe thee now.

HELLENA.

Well, I see our business as well as humours are alike; yours to
cozen as many maids as will trust you, and I as many men as have
faith — see if I have not as desperate a lying look as you can have
for the heart of you.   185

Pulls off her vizard: he starts.

— How do you like it, captain?

WILLMORE.

Like it! By heaven, I never saw so much beauty! Oh the charms of
those sprightly black eyes! That strangely fair face, full of smiles

and dimples! Those soft round melting cherry lips! And small
even white teeth! Not to be expressed, but silently adored! Oh,   190
one look more! And strike me dumb, or I shall repeat nothing
else till I'm mad.

He seems to court her to pull off her vizard: she refuses.

ANGELLICA.

I can endure no more — nor is it fit to interrupt him, for if I do,
my jealousy has so destroyed my reason, I shall undo him —
therefore I'll retire — [*To one of her bravoes.*] and you, Sebastian,   195
follow that woman, and learn who 'tis; [*To the other bravo.*] while
you tell the fugitive, I would speak to him instantly.

Exit.

*This while Florinda is talking to Belvile, who stands sullenly. Frederick
courting Valeria.*

VALERIA.

Prithee, dear stranger, be not so sullen, for though you have lost
your love, you see my friend frankly offers you hers to play with
in the meantime.   200

BELVILE.

Faith, madam, I am sorry I can't play at her game.

FREDERICK.

Pray leave your intercession, and mind your own affair. They'll
better agree apart; he's a modest sigher in company, but alone
no woman scapes him.

FLORINDA.

Sure he does but rally — yet if it should be true — I'll tempt him   205
farther. Believe me, noble stranger, I'm no common mistress,
and for a little proof on't, wear this jewel — nay, take it, sir, 'tis
right, and bills of exchange may sometimes miscarry.

BELVILE.

Madam, why am I chose out of all mankind to be the object of
your bounty?   210

---

208 bills of exchange] written promises of future payment

VALERIA.

There's another civil question asked.

FREDERICK.

Pox of's modesty, it spoils his own markets and hinders mine.

FLORINDA.

Sir, from my window, I have often seen you, and women of my quality have so few opportunities for love, that we ought to lose[†] none.

215

FREDERICK.

Ay, this is something! Here's a woman! When shall I be blessed with so much kindness from your fair mouth?

[*Aside to Belvile*] — Take the jewel, fool.

BELVILE.

You tempt me strangely, madam, every way —

FLORINDA. [*Aside.*]

So, if I find him false, my whole repose is gone.

220

BELVILE.

And but for a vow I've made to a very fair[†] lady, this goodness has subdued me.

FREDERICK.

Pox on't, be kind, in pity to me be kind, for I am to thrive here but as you treat her friend.

HELLENA.

Tell me what you did in yonder house, and I'll unmask.

225

WILLMORE.

Yonder house — oh — I went to — a — to — why, there's a friend of mine lives there.

HELLENA.

What, a she, or a he friend?

WILLMORE.

A man, upon honour! A man — a she friend — no, no, madam, you have done my business I thank you.

230

HELLENA.

And was't your man friend that had more darts in's eyes than Cupid carries in's whole budget of arrows?

WILLMORE.

So —

---

232 budget] wallet, leather bag

HELLENA.

Ah, such a bona roba! To be in her arms is lying in fresco, all perfumed air about me — was this your man friend too?   235

WILLMORE.

So —

HELLENA.

That gave you the he and the she gold, that begets young pleasures?

WILLMORE.

Well, well, madam, then you see there are ladies in the world that
will not be cruel — there are, madam, there are —   240

HELLENA.

And there be men too, as fine, wild, inconstant fellows as yourself, there be, captain, there be, if you go to that now — therefore
I'm resolved —

WILLMORE.

Oh!

HELLENA.

To see your face no more —   245

WILLMORE.

Oh!

HELLENA.

Till tomorrow.

WILLMORE.

Egad, you frighted me.

HELLENA.

Nor then neither, unless you'll swear never to see that lady more.

WILLMORE.

See her! — Why, never to think of womankind again.   250

HELLENA.

Kneel — and swear —

Kneels, she gives him her hand.

WILLMORE.

I do, never to think — to see — to love — nor lie — with any but
thy self.

HELLENA.

Kiss the book.

WILLMORE.

Oh, most religiously.   255

Kisses her hand.

HELLENA.

Now what a wicked creature am I, to damn a proper fellow.

CALLIS. [*To Florinda.*]

Madam, I'll stay no longer, 'tis e'en dark.

FLORINDA.

However sir, I'll leave this with you — that when I'm gone, you may repent the opportunity you have lost by your modesty.

Gives him the jewel which is her picture, and exits. He gazes after her.

WILLMORE.

'Twill be an age till tomorrow — and till then I will most impa-   260
tiently expect you. Adieu, my dear pretty angel.

Exeunt all the women.

BELVILE.

Ha! Florinda's picture — 'twas she herself — what a dull dog was I!
I would have given the world for one minute's discourse with her.

FREDERICK.

This comes of your modesty! Ah, pox o' your vow, 'twas ten to
one, but we had lost the jewel by't.   265

BELVILE.

Willmore! The blessed'st opportunity lost! Florinda! Friends!
Florinda!

WILLMORE.

Ah rogue! Such black eyes! Such a face! Such a mouth! Such
teeth! And so much wit!

BELVILE.

All, all, and a thousand charms besides.   270

WILLMORE.

Why, dost thou know her?

BELVILE.

Know her! Ay, ay, and a pox take me with all my heart for being
modest.

WILLMORE.

But harkee, friend of mine, are you my rival? And have I been
only beating the bush all this while?   275

BELVILE.

I understand thee not — I'm mad — see here —

Shows the picture.

WILLMORE.

Ha! Whose picture's this? 'Tis a fine wench!

FREDERICK.

The colonel's mistress,[†] sir.

WILLMORE.

Oh, oh, here — I thought't had been another prize — come, come, a bottle will set thee right again.

280

Gives the picture back.

BELVILE.

I am content to try, and by that time 'twill be late enough for our design.

WILLMORE.

Agreed.
Love does all day the soul's great empire keep
But wine at night lulls the soft god asleep.

285

Exeunt.

Scene II.
Lucetta's House.

III.ii

has no heart.

Enter Blunt and Lucetta with a light.

LUCETTA.

Now we are safe and free; no fears of the coming home of my old jealous husband, which made me a little thoughtful when you came in first — but now love is all the business of my soul.

BLUNT. [*Aside.*]

I am transported! Pox on't, that I had but some fine things to say to her, such as lovers use — I was a fool not to learn of Frederick a little by heart before I came — something I must say —

5

— 'Sheartlikins, sweet soul! I am not used to compliment, but I'm an honest gentleman, and thy humble servant.

LUCETTA.

I have nothing to pay for so great a favour, but such a love as
cannot but be great, since at first sight of that sweet face and   10
shape, it made me your absolute captive.

BLUNT.

Kind heart! How prettily she talks! [*Aside.*] Egad, I'll show her
husband a Spanish trick; send him out of the world and marry
her. She's damnably in love with me, and will ne'er mind settle-
ments, and so there's that saved.   15

LUCETTA.

Well sir, I'll go and undress me, and be with you instantly.

BLUNT.

Make haste then, for 'sheartlikins, dear soul, thou canst not guess
at the pain of a longing lover, when his joys are drawn within the
compass of a few minutes.

LUCETTA.

You speak my sense, and I'll make haste to prove it.   20

Exit.

BLUNT.

'Tis a rare girl! And this one night's enjoyment with her will be
worth all the days I ever passed in Essex. Would she would go
with me into England; though to say truth, there's plenty of
whores already. But a pox on 'em, they are such mercenary —
prodigal whores, that they want such a one as this that's free and   25
generous to give 'em good examples. Why, what a house she has,
how rich and fine!

Enter Sancho†

SANCHO.

Sir, my lady has sent me to conduct you to her chamber.

---

14 settlements] financial arrangements which are part of a marriage contract

BLUNT.

Sir, I shall be proud to follow — here's one of her servants too! 'Sheartlikins, by this garb and gravity, he might be a justice of peace in Essex, and is but a pimp here.

30

Exeunt.

Scene III

The scene changes to a chamber with an alcove bed in't, a table, etc. Lucetta in bed. Enter Sancho and Blunt, who takes the candle of Sancho at the door.

SANCHO.

Sir, my commission reaches no farther.

BLUNT.

Sir, I'll excuse your compliment — what, in bed my sweet mistress?

LUCETTA.

You see, I still outdo you in kindness.

BLUNT.

And thou shalt see what haste I'll make to quit scores — oh, the luckiest rogue!

5

He undresses himself.

LUCETTA.

Should you be false or cruel now!

BLUNT.

False! 'Sheartlikins, what dost thou take me for? A Jew? An insensible heathen? A pox of thy old jealous husband; an he were dead, egad, sweet soul, it should be none of my fault if I did not marry thee.

10

LUCETTA.

It never should be mine.

BLUNT.

Good soul! I'm the fortunatest dog!

---

9 an] if

LUCETTA.

Are you not undressed yet?

BLUNT.

As much as my impatience will permit.   15

Goes toward the bed in his shirt, drawers, etc.†

LUCETTA.

Hold, sir, put out the light, it may betray us else.

BLUNT.

Anything, I need no other light but that of thine eyes! 'Sheartlikins, there I think I had it.

Puts out the candle, the bed descends, he gropes about to find it.

— Why — why — where am I got? What, not yet? Where are you
sweetest? Ah, the rogue's silent now — a pretty love-trick this —   20
how she'll laugh at me anon! You need not, my dear rogue! You
need not! I'm all on fire already — come, come, now call me in
pity. Sure I'm enchanted! I have been round the chamber, and
can find neither woman, nor bed — I locked the door, I'm sure
she cannot go that way — or if she could, the bed could not.   25
Enough, enough, my pretty wanton, do not carry the jest too far —
[*Lights on a trap, and is let down.*] Ha, betrayed! Dogs! Rogues!
Pimps! Help! Help!

Enter Lucetta, Phillippo, and Sancho with a light.

PHILLIPPO.

Ha, ha, ha, he's dispatched† finely.

LUCETTA.

Now, sir, had I been coy, we had missed of this booty.   30

PHILLIPPO.

Nay, when I saw't was a substantial fool, I was mollified; but
when you dote upon a serenading coxcomb, upon a face, fine
clothes, and a lute, it makes me rage.

Stage Direction: bed descends] presumably through a trap door; possibly the same trap
   Blunt falls through a few lines later

LUCETTA.

You know I was never guilty of that folly, my dear Phillippo, but with yourself — but come, let's see what we have got by this. 35

PHILLIPPO.

A rich coat! Sword and hat — these breeches, too, are well lined — see here, a gold watch! A purse — ha! Gold! At least two hundred pistoles! A bunch of diamond rings! And one with the family arms! A gold box — with a medal of his king! And his lady mother's picture! These were sacred relics, believe me. See, the 40 waistband of his breeches have a mine of gold! Old Queen Bess's, we have a quarrel to her ever since eighty-eight, and may therefore justify the theft; the Inquisition might have committed it.

LUCETTA.

See, a bracelet of bowed † gold! These his sisters tied about his 45 arm at parting — but well — for all this, I fear his being a stranger may make a noise and hinder our trade with them hereafter.

PHILLIPPO.

That's our security; he is not only a stranger to us, but to the country too — the common shore† into which he is descended, thou knowst conducts him into another street, which this light 50 will hinder him from ever finding again — he knows neither your name, nor that of the street where your house is, nay nor the way to his own lodgings.

LUCETTA.

And art not thou an unmerciful rogue! Not to afford him one night for all this? I should not have been such a Jew. 55

---

41 old Queen Bess] Queen Elizabeth I, who reigned from 1558-1603
42 eighty-eight] In 1588 the Spanish Armada advanced towards England. In England the Armada was seen as a triumph of English sea-power, although a storm wrecked and dispersed many of the Spanish galleons.
45 bowed] bent, braided (?)

PHILLIPPO.

Blame me not, Lucetta, to keep as much of thee as I can to myself — come, that thought makes me wanton! Let's to bed! Sancho, lock up these.
This is the fleece which fools do bear
Designed for witty men to shear.   60

Exeunt.

Scene IV   III.iv

The scene changes and discovers Blunt, creeping out of a common shore, his
face, etc. all dirty.

BLUNT.

Oh lord!

Climbing up.

I am got out at last, and (which is a miracle) without a clue — and
now to damning and cursing — but if that would ease me, where
shall I begin? With my fortune, myself, or the quean that cozened
me? What a dog was I to believe in woman! Oh coxcomb! Igno-   5
rant conceited coxcomb! To fancy she could be enamoured with
my person! At first sight enamoured! Oh, I'm a cursed puppy!
'Tis plain, "fool" was writ upon my forehead! She perceived it —
saw the Essex calf there — for what allurements could there be in
this countenance, which I can endure, because I'm acquainted   10
with it — oh, dull silly dog! To be thus soothed into a cozening!
Had I been drunk, I might fondly have credited the young
quean! But as I was in my right wits, to be thus cheated confirms
it I am a dull, believing, English country fop — but my comrades!
Death and the devil! There's the worst of all — then a ballad will   15
be sung tomorrow on the prado, to a lousy tune of "The Enchanted 'Squire, and the Annihilated Damsel" — but Frederick,

---

2 clue] ball of thread used as a guide out of a maze; also "clew"
4 quean] prostitute
16 prado] field, lawn, meadow (Sp.)

that rogue, and the colonel, will abuse me beyond all Christian
patience — had she left me my clothes, I have a bill of exchange
at home would have saved my credit — but now all hope is taken   20
from me — well, I'll home (if I can find the way) with this consola-
tion, that I am not the first kind, believing coxcomb; but there
are, gallants, many such good natures amongst ye.
And though you've better arts to hide your follies,
Adsheartlikins y'are all as errant cullies.   25

Exit.[†]

Scene V, the Garden in the Night   III.v

Enter Florinda in an undress, with a key and a little box.

FLORINDA.
Well, thus far I'm on my way to happiness. I have got myself free
from Callis; my brother too, I find by yonder light, is got into his
cabinet, and thinks not of me; I have by good fortune got the key
of the garden back-door. I'll open it to prevent Belvile's knocking
— a little noise will now alarm my brother. Now am I as fearful as   5
a young thief.

Unlocks the door.

Hark — what noise is that? Oh, 'twas the wind that played
amongst the boughs — Belvile stays long, methinks — it's time —
stay — for fear of a surprise, I'll hide these jewels in yonder jes-
samin..   10

She goes to lay down the box.

---

25 cullies] fools; dupes
Stage Direction: undress] casual dress or robe worn at home
3 cabinet] small private room
9 jessamin] jasmine

Enter Willmore drunk.

WILLMORE.

What the devil is become of these fellows, Belvile and Frederick?
They promised to stay at the next corner for me, but who the
devil knows the corner of a full moon — now — whereabouts am
I? Hah — what have we here, a garden! A very convenient place
to sleep in — hah — what has God sent us here! A female! By this   15
light a woman! I'm a dog if it be not a very wench!

FLORINDA.

He's come! Hah — who's there?

WILLMORE.

Sweet soul! Let me salute thy shoe-string.

FLORINDA.

'Tis not my Belvile — good heavens! I know him not — who are
you, and from whence come you?   20

WILLMORE.

Prithee — prithee child — not so many questions — let it suffice I
am here, child — come, come kiss me.

FLORINDA.

Good gods! What luck is mine?

WILLMORE.

Only good luck, child, parlous good luck — come hither — 'tis a
delicate shining wench — by this hand she's perfumed, and smells   25
like any nosegay — prithee, dear soul, let's not play the fool, and
lose time — precious time — for as gad shall save me, I'm as honest a fellow as breathes, though I'm a little disguised at present —
come I say. Why, thou may'st be free with me, I'll be very secret.
I'll not boast who 'twas obliged me, not I — for hang me if I know   30
thy name.

FLORINDA.

Heavens! What a filthy beast is this?

WILLMORE.

I am so, and thou ought'st the sooner to lie with me for that reason — for look you child, there will be no sin in't, because 'twas
neither designed nor premeditated. 'Tis pure accident on both   35

---

24 parlous] extremely
28 disguised] drunk

sides — that's a certain thing now. Indeed should I make love to
you, and you vow fidelity — and swear and lie till you believed
and yielded — that were to make it wilful fornication, the crying
sin of the nation. Thou art therefore (as thou art a good Christian) obliged in conscience to deny me nothing. Now — come be   40
kind without any more idle prating.

FLORINDA.

Oh I am ruined — wicked man, unhand me.

WILLMORE.

Wicked! Egad child, a judge, were he young and vigorous and
saw those eyes of thine, would know 'twas they gave the first blow
— the first provocation — come prithee, let's lose no time, I say —   45
this is a fine convenient place.

FLORINDA.

Sir, let me go, I conjure you, or I'll call out.

WILLMORE.

Ay, ay, you were best to call witness to see how finely you treat
me — do —

FLORINDA.

I'll cry murder, rape, or anything if you do not instantly let me   50
go.

WILLMORE.

A rape! Come, come, you lie, you baggage, you lie. What, I'll warrant you would fain have the world believe now that you are not
so forward as I. No, not you. Why, at this time of night, was your
cobweb door set open, dear spider — but to catch flies? Hah —
come — or I shall be damnably angry. Why, what a coil is here —   55

FLORINDA.

Sir, can you think —

WILLMORE.

That you would do't for nothing — oh, oh, I find what you would
be at — look here's a pistole† for you — here's a work indeed —
here — take it I say —   ↑ he'll pay her.

FLORINDA.

For heavens sake, sir, as you're a gentleman —   60

---

55 coil] turmoil, fuss

WILLMORE.

So — now — now — she would be wheedling me for more — what, you will not take it then — you are resolved you will not — come — come take it or I'll put it up again — for look ye, I never give more. Why how now, mistress, are you so high i'th'mouth a pistole† won't down with you — hah — why, what a works here — in good time — come, no struggling to be gone — but an y'are good at a dumb wrestle I'm for ye — look ye — I'm for ye —

65

She struggles with him.

Enter Belvile and Frederick.

BELVILE.

The door is open. A pox of this mad fellow; I'm angry that we've lost him; I durst have sworn he had followed us.

FREDERICK.

But you were so hasty, colonel to be gone.

70

FLORINDA.

Help! Help! Murder! Help — oh, I am ruined.

BELVILE.

Ha! Sure that's Florinda's voice.

Comes up to them.

A man! Villain, let go that lady!

A noise. Willmore turns and draws, Frederick interposes.

FLORINDA.

Belvile! Heavens! My brother too is coming, and 'twill be impossible to escape — Belvile, I conjure you to walk under my chamber window, from whence I'll give you some instructions what to do — this rude man has undone us.

75

Exit.

---

66 an] if

WILLMORE.
Belvile!

Enter Pedro, Stephano, and other servants with lights.

PEDRO.
I'm betrayed! Run, Stephano, and see if Florinda be safe.

Exit Stephano.

So, whoe'er they be, all is not well. I'll to Florinda's chamber.   80

They fight and Pedro's party beats 'em out. Going out, meets Stephano.

STEPHANO.
You need not, sir; the poor lady's fast asleep and thinks no harm.
I would not awake her sir, for fear of frighting her with your danger.
PEDRO.
I'm glad she's there — rascals, how came the garden door open?
STEPHANO.
That question comes too late, sir; some of my fellow servants   85
masquerading, I'll warrant.
PEDRO.
Masquerading! A lewd custom to debauch our youth — there's
something more in this then, I imagine.

Exeunt.

Scene VI   III.vi

Scene changes to the street.

Enter Belvile in rage, Frederick holding him, and Willmore melancholy.

WILLMORE.
Why, how the devil should I know Florinda?
BELVILE.
A plague of your ignorance! If it had not been Florinda, must
you be a beast? A brute? A senseless swine?

WILLMORE.

    Well, sir, you see I am endued with patience – I can bear –
though egad, y'are very free with me, methinks. I was in good   5
hopes the quarrel would have been on my side, for so uncivilly
interrupting me.

BELVILE.

    Peace, brute! Whilst thou'rt safe – oh, I'm distracted.

WILLMORE.

    Nay, nay, I'm an unlucky dog, that's certain.

BELVILE.

    Ah, curse upon the star that ruled my birth! Or whatsoever other   10
influence that makes me still so wretched.

WILLMORE.

    Thou break'st my heart with these complaints. There is no star in
fault, no influence but sack, the cursed sack I drunk.

FREDERICK.

    Why how the devil came you so drunk?

WILLMORE.

    Why how the devil came you so sober?   15

BELVILE.

    A curse upon his thin skull, he was always before hand that way.

FREDERICK.

    Prithee, dear colonel, forgive him, he's sorry for his fault.

BELVILE.

    He's always so after he has done a mischief – a plague on all such
brutes.

WILLMORE.

    By this light, I took her for an errant harlot.   20

BELVILE.

    Damn your debauched opinion! Tell me sot, had'st thou so much
sense and light about thee to distinguish her woman, and
could'st not see something about her face and person, to strike
an awful reverence into thy soul?

WILLMORE.

    Faith no, I considered her as mere a woman as I could wish.   25

BELVILE.

    'Sdeath, I have no patience – draw, or I'll kill you.

---

4 endued] equipped, supplied

WILLMORE.

Let that alone till tomorrow, and if I set not all right again, use
your pleasure.

BELVILE.

Tomorrow! Damn it.

The spiteful† light will lead me to no happiness.   30

Tomorrow is Antonio's, and perhaps

Guides him to my undoing – oh, that I could meet

This rival! This pow'rful fortunate!

WILLMORE.

What then?

BELVILE.

Let thy own reason, or my rage, instruct thee.   35

WILLMORE.

I shall be finely informed then, no doubt; hear me, colonel –
hear me – show me the man and I'll do his business.

BELVILE.

I know him no more than thou, or if I did I should not need thy
aid.

WILLMORE.

This, you say, is Angellica's house. I promised the kind baggage   40
to lie with her tonight.

Offers to go in.

Enter Antonio and his page. Antonio knocks on the hilt of's sword.

ANTONIO.

You paid the thousand crowns I directed?

PAGE.

To the lady's old woman, sir, I did.

WILLMORE.

Who the devil have we here!

BELVILE.

I'll now plant myself under Florinda's window, and if I find no   45
comfort there, I'll die.

Exeunt Belvile and Frederick.

Enter Moretta.

MORETTA.
Page!
PAGE.
Here's my lord.
WILLMORE.
How is this! A picaroon going to board my frigate? Here's one
chase gun for you.   50

*Drawing his sword, justles Antonio who turns and draws. They fight,
Antonio falls.*

MORETTA.
Oh bless us! We're all undone!

Runs in and shuts the door.

PAGE.
Help! Murder!

Belvile returns at the noise of the fighting.

BELVILE.
Ha! The mad rogue's engaged in some unlucky adventure again.

arrested.   *Enter two or three masqueraders.*

MASQUERADERS.
Ha! A man killed!
WILLMORE.
How! A man killed! Then I'll go home to sleep.   55

Puts up and reels out. Exeunt masqueraders another way.

BELVILE.
Who should it be! Pray heaven the rogue is safe, for all my quarrel to him.   *truly constant
to Florinda*

Stage Direction: justles] jostles

[III.v]

As Belvile is groping about, enter an officer and six soldiers.

SOLDIER.
Who's there?
OFFICER.
So here's one dispatched — secure the murderer.

Soldiers seize on Belvile.

BELVILE.
Do not mistake my charity for murder!   60
I came to his assistance.
OFFICER.
That shall be tried, sir — St. Jago, swords drawn in carnival time!

Goes to Antonio.

ANTONIO.
Thy hand, prithee.
OFFICER.
Ha! Don Antonio! Look well to the villain there. How is it, sir?
ANTONIO.
I'm hurt.   65
BELVILE.
Has my humanity made me a criminal?
OFFICER.
Away with him.
BELVILE.
What a cursed chance is this?

Exeunt soldiers with Belvile.

ANTONIO. [*To the officer.*]
This is the man that has set upon me twice — carry him to my
apartment, till you have farther orders from me.   70

Exit Antonio led.

---

62 St. Jago] St. James the Apostle

ACT IV.

Scene I. A fine room.

Discovers Belvile as by dark alone.

BELVILE.

When shall I be weary of railing on fortune, who is resolved
never to turn with smiles upon me? Two such defeats in one
night — none but the devil and that mad rogue could have con-
trived to have plagued me with. I am here a prisoner — but where
— heaven knows — and if there be murder done, I can soon de- 5
cide the fate of a stranger in a nation without mercy. Yet this is
nothing to the torture my soul bows with when I think of losing
my fair, my dear, Florinda — hark — my door opens — a light — a
man — and seems of quality — armed too! Now shall I die like a
dog without defence. 10

*Enter Antonio in a nightgown with a light; his arm in a scarf, and a sword
under his arm. He sets the candle on the table.*

ANTONIO.

Sir, I come to know what injuries I have done you that could pro-
voke you to so mean an action as to attack me basely, without al-
lowing time for my defence?

BELVILE.

Sir, for a man in my circumstances to plead innocence would
look like fear — but view me well, and you will find no marks of 15
coward on me; nor anything that betrays that brutality you ac-
cuse me with.

ANTONIO.

In vain, sir, you impose upon my sense.
You are not only he who drew on me last night,
But yesterday before the same house, that of Angellica. 20
Yet there is something in your face and mien
That makes me wish I were mistaken.

Stage Direction: nightgown] robe, dressing gown
21 mien] appearance, look

BELVILE.

    I own I fought today in the defence of a friend of mine, with
    whom you (if you're the same) and your party were first engaged.
    Perhaps you think this crime enough to kill me,   25
    But if you do, I cannot fear you'll do it basely.

ANTONIO.

    No, sir, I'll make you fit for a defence with this.

Gives him the sword.

BELVILE.

    This gallantry surprises me — nor know I how to use this present,
    sir, against a man so brave.

ANTONIO.

    You shall not need.   30
    For know, I come to snatch you from a danger
    That is decreed against you;
    Perhaps your life, or long imprisonment;
    And 'twas with so much courage you offended,
    I cannot see you punished.   35

BELVILE.

    How shall I pay this generosity?

ANTONIO.

    It had been safer to have killed another
    Than have attempted me.
    To show your danger, sir, I'll let you know my quality;
    And 'tis the viceroy's son whom you have wounded.   40

BELVILE. [*Aside.*]

    The viceroy's son!
    Death and confusion! Was this plague reserved
    To complete all the rest? Obliged by him!
    The man of all the world I would destroy.

ANTONIO.

    You seem disordered, sir.   45

BELVILE.

    Yes, trust me sir, I am, and 'tis with pain
    That man receives such bounties,
    Who wants the pow'r to pay 'em back again.

ANTONIO.

    To gallant spirits 'tis indeed uneasy;
    But you may quickly overpay me, sir.   50

BELVILE.

    Then I am well.

    [*Aside.*] Kind heav'n, but set us even,

    That I may fight with him and keep my honour safe.

    — Oh, I'm impatient, sir, to be discounting the mighty debt I owe

    you; command me quickly —   55

ANTONIO.

    I have a quarrel with a rival, sir,

    About the maid we love.

BELVILE.   [*Aside.*]

    Death, 'tis Florinda he means —

    That thought destroys my reason,

    And I shall kill him —   60

ANTONIO.

    My rival, sir,

    Is one has all the virtues man can boast of.

BELVILE.   [*Aside.*]

    Death! Who should this be?

ANTONIO.[†]

    He challenged me to meet him on the Molo

    As soon as day appeared; but last night's quarrel   65

    Has made my arm unfit to guide a sword.

BELVILE.

    I apprehend you, sir; you'd have me kill the man

    That lays a claim to the maid you speak of.

    I'll do't — I'll fly to do't!

ANTONIO.

    Sir, do you know her?   70

BELVILE.

    No, sir, but 'tis enough she is admired by you.

ANTONIO.

    Sir, I shall rob you of the glory on't,

    For you must fight under my name and dress.

BELVILE.

    That opinion must be strangely obliging that makes

    You think I can personate the brave Antonio,   75

    Whom I can but strive to imitate.

ANTONIO.

    You say too much to my advantage.

    Come, sir, the day appears that calls you forth.

    Within, sir, is the habit.

Exit Antonio.

BELVILE.

Fantastic fortune, thou deceitful light,   80
That cheats the wearied traveller by night,
Though on a precipice each step you tread,
I am resolved to follow where you lead.

Exit.

Scene II, The Molo.   IV.ii

Enter Florinda and Callis in masks with Stephano.

FLORINDA. [*Aside.*]
I'm dying with my fears; Belvile's not coming as I expected under
my window, makes me believe that all those fears are true.
— Canst thou not tell with whom my brother fights?
STEPHANO.
No, madam, they were both in masquerade. I was by when they
challenged one another, and they had decided the quarrel then,   5
but were prevented by some cavaliers, which made 'em put it off
till now — but I am sure 'tis about you they fight.
FLORINDA. [*Aside.*]
Nay, then 'tis with Belvile, for what other lover have I that dares
fight for me, except Antonio? And he is too much in favour with
my brother. If it be he, for whom shall I direct my prayers to   10
heaven?
STEPHANO.
Madam, I must leave you, for if my master see me, I shall be
hanged for being your conductor. I† escaped narrowly for the excuse I made for you last night i'th'garden.
FLORINDA.
And I'll reward thee for't — prithee no more.   15

Exit Stephano.

Enter Don Pedro in his masquing habit.

PEDRO.
Antonio's late today; the place will fill, and we may be prevented.

Walks about.

FLORINDA.   [*Aside.*]
"Antonio" — sure I heard amiss.
PEDRO.
But who will not excuse a happy lover
When soft fair arms confine the yielding neck,
And the kind whisper languishingly breathes,   20
"Must you begone so soon?"
Sure I had dwelt for ever on her bosom.
But stay, he's here.

Enter Belvile dressed in Antonio's clothes.

FLORINDA. ——> thinks its Antonio.
'Tis not Belvile; half my fears are vanisht.
PEDRO.
Antonio!   25
BELVILE.   [*Aside.*]
This must be he.
— You're early, sir — I do not use to be outdone this way.
PEDRO.
The wretched, sir, are watchful, and 'tis enough
You've the advantage of me in Angellica.
BELVILE.   [*Aside.*]
Angellica! Or I've mistook my man or else Antonio.   30
Can he forget his interest in Florinda,
And fight for common prize?
PEDRO.
Come, sir, you know our terms —
BELVILE.   [*Aside.*]
By heav'n not I.
— No talking, I am ready, sir.   35

Offers to fight, Florinda runs in.

FLORINDA.   [*To Belvile.*]
Oh hold! Whoe'er you be, I do conjure you hold!

If you strike here — I die.

PEDRO.

Florinda!

BELVILE.

Florinda imploring for my rival!

PEDRO.

Away, this kindness is unreasonable. 40

Puts her by; they fight; she runs in just as Belvile disarms Pedro.

FLORINDA.

Who are you, sir, that dares deny my prayers?

BELVILE.

Thy prayers destroy him; if thou would'st preserve him,
Do that thou'rt unacquainted with and curse him.

She holds him.

FLORINDA.

By all you hold most dear, by her you love,
I do conjure you, touch him not. 45

BELVILE.

By her I love!
See — I obey — and at your feet resign
The useless trophy of my victory.

Lays his sword at her feet.

PEDRO.

Antonio, you've done enough to prove you love Florinda.

BELVILE.

Love Florinda! 50
Does heav'n love adoration, prayer or penitence! Love her! Here,
sir — your sword again.

Snatches up the sword and gives it him.

Upon this truth I'll fight my life away.

PEDRO.

No, you've redeemed my sister, and my friendship!

He gives him Florinda and pulls off his vizard to show his face and puts it on again.

BELVILE.

 Don Pedro! 55

PEDRO.

 Can you resign your claims to other women,

 And give your heart entirely to Florinda?

BELVILE.

 Entire as dying saints' confessions are.

 I can delay my happiness no longer.

 This minute let me make Florinda mine! 60

PEDRO.

 This minute let it be — no time so proper.

 This night my father will arrive from Rome,

 And possibly may hinder what we purpose!

FLORINDA.

 Oh heavens! This minute!

Enter masqueraders and pass over.

BELVILE.

 Oh, do not ruin me! 65

PEDRO.

 The place begins to fill, and that we may not be observed, do you walk off to St. Peter's church, where I will meet you, and conclude your happiness.

BELVILE.

 I'll meet you there.

 [*Aside.*] — If there be no more saints' churches in Naples. 70

FLORINDA.

 Oh, stay sir, and recall your hasty doom!

 Alas, I have not yet prepared my heart

 To entertain so strange a guest.

PEDRO.

 Away, this silly modesty is assumed too late.

BELVILE.

 Heaven, madam! What do you do? 75

FLORINDA.

 Do! Despise the man that lays a tyrant's claim

 To what he ought to conquer by submission.

BELVILE.
    You do not know me — move a little this way.

                        Draws her aside.

FLORINDA.
    Yes, you may force me even to the altar,
    But not the holy man that offers there   80
    Shall force me to be thine.

                Pedro talks to Callis this while.

BELVILE.
    Oh do not lose[†] so blest an opportunity —
    See — 'tis your Belvile — not Antonio,
    Whom your mistaken scorn and anger ruins.

                    Pulls off his vizard.

FLORINDA.
    Belvile!   85
    Where was my soul it could not meet thy voice
    And take this knowledge in?

        As they are talking, enter Willmore, finely dressed, and Frederick.

WILLMORE. —> reveals Belvile identity.
    No intelligence, no news of Belvile yet — well, I am the most un-
    lucky rascal in nature — ha — am I deceived? Or is it he? Look
    Fred — 'tis he — my dear Belvile!   90

        Runs and embraces him. Belvile's vizard falls out on's hand.

BELVILE.
    Hell and confusion seize thee!
PEDRO.
    Ha! Belvile! I beg your pardon sir.

                Takes Florinda from him.

BELVILE.

    Nay, touch her not. She's mine by conquest, sir;

    I won her by my sword.

WILLMORE.

    Did'st thou so — and egad, child, we'll keep her by the sword.   95

Draws on Pedro. Belvile goes between.

BELVILE.

    Stand off!

    Thou'rt so profanely lewd, so curst by heaven,

    All quarrels thou espousest must be fatal.

WILLMORE.

    Nay, an you be so hot, my valour's coy, and shall be courted

    when you want it next.   100

Puts up his sword.

BELVILE.   [*To Pedro.*]

    You know I ought to claim a victor's right.

    But you're the brother to divine Florinda,

    To whom I'm such a slave — to purchase her,

    I durst not hurt the man she holds so dear.

PEDRO.

    'Twas by Antonio's, not by Belvile's sword   105

    This question should have been decided, sir.

    I must confess, much to your bravery's due,

    Both now, and when I met you last in arms.

    But I am nicely punctual in my word,

    As men of honour ought, and beg your pardon.   110

    For this mistake another time shall clear.

Aside to Florinda as they are going out.

    This was some plot between you and Belvile.

    But I'll prevent you.

Belvile looks after her and begins to walk up and down in rage.

WILLMORE.

Do not be modest now and lose[†] the woman, but if we shall fetch
her back so —   115

BELVILE.

Do not speak to me —

WILLMORE.

Not speak to you — egad, I'll speak to you, and will be answered,
too.

BELVILE.

Will you, sir —

WILLMORE.

I know I've done some mischief, but I'm so dull a puppy, that I'm   120
the son of a whore if I know how, or where — prithee inform my
understanding —

BELVILE.

Leave me, I say, and leave me instantly.

WILLMORE.

I will not leave you in this humour, nor till I know my crime.

BELVILE.

Death, I'll tell you sir —   125

Draws and runs at Willmore. He runs out, Belvile after him;
Frederick interposes.

Enter Angellica, Moretta and Sebastian.

ANGELLICA.

Ha — Sebastian —
Is not that Willmore? Haste[†] — haste and bring him back.

FREDERICK.

The colonel's mad — I never saw him thus before. I'll after 'em
lest he do some mischief, for I am sure Willmore will not draw
on him.   130

Exit.

ANGELLICA.

I am all rage! My first desires defeated!
For one for aught[†] he knows that has no
Other merit than her quality,
Her being Don Pedro's sister — he loves her!

I know 'tis so — dull, dull, insensible — 135
He will not see me now though oft invited,
And broke his word last night — false perjured man!
He that but yesterday fought for my favours,
And would have made his life a sacrifice
To've gained one night with me, 140
Must now be hired and courted to my arms.

MORETTA.

I told you what would come on't, but Moretta's an old doting
fool. Why did you give him five hundred crowns, but to set himself out for other lovers? You should have kept him poor if you
had meant to have had any good from him. 145

ANGELLICA.

Oh, name not such mean trifles — had I given him all
My youth has earned from sin,
I had not lost a thought, nor sigh upon't.
But I have given him my eternal rest,
My whole repose, my future joys, my heart! 150
My virgin heart, Moretta! Oh, 'tis gone!

MORETTA.

Curse on him, here he comes;
How fine she has made him too.

Enter Willmore and Sebastian; Angellica turns and walks away.

WILLMORE.

How now, turned shadow!
Fly when I pursue and follow when I fly! 155

Sings.

Stay, gentle shadow of my dove
And tell me ere I go,
Whether the substance may not prove
A fleeting thing like you.

There's a soft kind look remaining yet. 160

As she turns she looks on him.

ANGELLICA.

Well sir, you may be gay; all happiness, all joys, pursue you still. Fortune's your slave, and gives you every hour choice of new hearts and beauties, till you are cloyed with the repeated bliss which others vainly languish for.

[*Aside*]‡ But know, false man, that I shall be revenged.   165

Turns away in rage.

WILLMORE.

So, gad, there are of those faint-hearted lovers, whom such a sharp lesson next their hearts would make as impotent as four-score. Pox o' this whining. My business is to laugh and love. A pox on't — I hate your sullen lover. A man shall lose as much time to put you in humour now, as would serve to gain a new   170 woman.

ANGELLICA.

I scorn to cool that fire I cannot raise,
Or do the drudgery of your virtuous mistress.

WILLMORE.

A virtuous mistress! Death, what a thing thou hast found out for me. Why, what the devil should I do with a virtuous woman? A   175 sort of ill-natured creatures, that take a pride to torment a lover. Virtue is but an infirmity in woman, a disease that renders even the handsome ungrateful; whilst the ill-favoured, for want of so-licitations and address, only fancy themselves so. I have lain with a woman of quality, who has all the while been railing at whores.   180

ANGELLICA.

I will not answer for your mistress's virtue,
Though she be young enough to know no guilt;
And I could wish you would persuade my heart
'Twas the two hundred thousand crowns you courted.

WILLMORE.

Two hundred thousand crowns! What story's this? What trick?   185
What woman? Ha!

ANGELLICA.

How strange you make it; have you forgot the creature you enter-tained on the piazza last night?

WILLMORE. [*Aside.*]

Ha! My gypsy worth two hundred thousand crowns! Oh, how I long to be with her — pox, I knew she was of quality.   190

ANGELLICA.

  False man! I see my ruin in thy face.

  How many vows you breathed upon my bosom,

  Never to be unjust — have you forgot so soon?

WILLMORE.

  Faith no, I was just coming to repeat 'em — but here's a humour

  indeed would make a man a saint. [*Aside.*] — Would she would   195

  be angry enough to leave me, and command me not to wait on

  her.

  Enter Hellena dressed in man's clothes.

HELLENA. [*Aside*] —> come to tell [*Wil of*] a woman who loves him. (her—)

  This must be Angellica! I know it by her mumping matron here.

  Ay, ay, 'tis she! My mad captain's with her too, for all his swear-

  ing — how this unconstant humour makes me love him!   200

  — Pray, good grave gentlewoman, is not this Angellica?

MORETTA.

  My too young sir, it is — [*Aside*]‡ I hope 'tis one from Don Anto-

  nio.

  Goes to Angellica.

HELLENA.   [*Aside.*]

  Well, something I'll do to vex him for this.

ANGELLICA.

  I will not speak with him; am I in humour to receive a lover?

WILLMORE.

  Not speak with him! Why I'll be gone and wait your idler minutes —   205

  can I show less obedience to the thing I love so fondly?

  Offers to go.

ANGELLICA.

  A fine excuse this! Stay —

---

198 mumping] mumbling, grimacing, sullen

WILLMORE.
    And hinder your advantage! Should I repay your bounties so un-
    gratefully?
ANGELLICA.
    Come hither, boy — that I may let you see   210
    How much above† the advantages you name
    I prize one minute's joy with you.
WILLMORE.
    Oh, you destroy me with this endearment.

                        Impatient to be gone.

    Death! How shall I get away? Madam, 'twill not be fit I should be
    seen with you — besides, it will not be convenient — and I've a   215
    friend — that's dangerously sick.
ANGELLICA.
    I see you're impatient — yet you shall stay.
WILLMORE.   [*Aside, and walks about impatiently.*]
    And miss my assignation with my gypsy.
HELLENA.
    Madam,

            Moretta brings Hellena, who addresses herself to Angellica.

    You'll hardly pardon my intrusion   220
    When you shall know my business,
    And I'm too young to tell my tale with art;
    But there must be a wondrous store of goodness,
    Where so much beauty dwells.
ANGELLICA.
    A pretty advocate, whoever sent thee.   225
    Prithee proceed — [*To Willmore, who is stealing off.*] — nay, sir, you
    shall not go.
WILLMORE.   [*Aside.*]
    Then I shall lose my dear gypsy for ever — pox on't, she stays me
    out of spite.
HELLENA.†
    I am related to a lady, madam,   230
    Young, rich, and nobly born, but has the fate
    To be in love with a young English gentleman.
    Strangely she loves him, at first sight she loved him,

But did adore him when she heard him speak;
For he, she said, had charms in every word,   235
That failed not to surprise, to wound and conquer.

WILLMORE. [*Aside.*]

Ha! Egad, I hope this concerns me.

ANGELLICA. [*Aside*]‡

'Tis my false man, he means — would he were gone.
This praise will raise his pride, and ruin me — [*To Willmore*]‡ Well
Since you are so impatient to be gone   240
I will release you, sir.

WILLMORE. [*Aside.*]

Nay, then, I'm sure 'twas me he spoke of; this cannot be the effects of kindness in her.
— No, madam, I've considered better on't, and will not give you cause of jealousy.   245

ANGELLICA.

But, sir, I've — business, that —

WILLMORE.

This shall not do; I know 'tis but to try me.

ANGELLICA.

Well, to your story, boy — [*Aside.*] though 'twill undo me.

HELLENA.

With this addition to his other beauties,
He won her unresisting tender heart.   250
He vowed, and sighed, and swore he loved her dearly;
And she believed the cunning flatterer,
And thought herself the happiest maid alive.
Today was the appointed time by both
To consummate their bliss,   255
The virgin, altar, and the priest were dressed
And whilst she languished for th'expected bridegroom,
She heard he paid his broken vows to you.

WILLMORE.

So, this is some dear rogue that's in love with me, and this way lets me know it; or if it be not me, he† means someone whose 260
place I may supply.

ANGELLICA.

Now I perceive
The cause of thy impatience to be gone,
And all the business of this glorious dress.

WILLMORE.
    Damn the young prater, I know not what he means.   265
HELLENA.
    Madam,
    In your fair eyes I read too much concern,
    To tell my farther business.
ANGELLICA.
    Prithee, sweet youth, talk on, thou mayest perhaps
    Raise here a storm that may undo my passion,   270
    And then I'll grant thee anything.
HELLENA.
    Madam, 'tis to entreat you (oh unreasonable),
    You would not see this stranger;
    For if you do, she vows you are undone,
    Though nature never made a man so excellent,   275
    And sure he'ad been a god, but for inconstancy.
WILLMORE.   [*Aside.*]
    Ah, rogue, how finely he's instructed!
    — 'Tis plain; some woman that has seen me *en passant*.
ANGELLICA.
    Oh, I shall burst with jealousy! Do you know the man you speak
    of?   280
HELLENA.
    Yes, madam, he used to be in buff and scarlet.
ANGELLICA.   [*To Willmore.*]
    Thou, false as hell, what canst thou say to this?
WILLMORE.
    By heaven —
ANGELLICA.
    Hold, do not damn thyself —
HELLENA.
    Nor hope to be believed.   285

He walks about, they follow.

---

265 prater] one who prates; i.e. talks foolishly or irrelevantly
278 *en passant*] in passing

ANGELLICA.

Oh perjured man!

Is't thus you pay my generous passion back?

HELLENA.

Why would you, sir, abuse my lady's faith?

ANGELLICA.

And use me so unhumanely.

HELLENA.

A maid so young, so innocent —   290

WILLMORE.

Ah, young devil.[†]

ANGELLICA.

Dost thou know thy life is in[†] my power?

HELLENA.

Or think my lady cannot be revenged?

WILLMORE. [*Aside.*]

So, so, the storm comes finely on.

ANGELLICA.

Now thou art silent, guilt has struck thee dumb.   295

Oh, hadst thou still been so, I'd lived in safety.

She turns away and weeps.

WILLMORE. [*Aside to Hellena; looks toward Angellica to watch her turning and as she comes towards them he meets her.*]

Sweetheart, the lady's name and house — quickly, I'm impatient to be with her.

HELLENA. [*Aside.*]

So, now is he for another woman.

WILLMORE.

The impudentest[†] young thing in nature,   300

I cannot persuade him out of his error, madam.

ANGELLICA.

I know he's in the right — yet thou'st a tongue

That would persuade him to deny his faith.

In rage walks away.

WILLMORE.

Her name, her name, dear boy —

Said softly to Hellena.

HELLENA.

    Have you forgot it, sir? 305

WILLMORE.   [*Aside.*]

    Oh, I perceive he's not to know I am a stranger to this lady.

    — Yes, yes, I do know — but I have forgot the —

Angellica turns.

    — By heaven such early confidence I never saw.

ANGELLICA.

    Did I not charge you with this mistress, sir?

    Which you denied, though I beheld your perjury. 310

    This little generosity of thine, has rendered back my heart.

Walks away.

WILLMORE.

    So, you have made sweet work here, my little mischief; look your
lady be kind and good-natured now, or I shall have but a cursed
bargain on't.

Angellica turns toward them.

    — The rogue's bred up to mischief; 315

    Art thou so great a fool to credit him?

ANGELLICA.

    Yes, I do, and you in vain impose upon me.

    Come hither, boy — is not this he you spake of?

HELLENA.

    I think — it is; I cannot swear, but I vow he has just such another
lying lover's look. 320

Hellena looks in his face, he gazes on her.

WILLMORE.

    Hah! Do not I know that face —

    [*Aside.*] By heaven, my little gypsy; what a dull dog was I,

    Had I but looked that way I'd known her.

    Are all my hopes of a new woman banished?

— Egad, if I do not fit thee for this, hang me. 325
— Madam, I have found out the plot.

HELLENA. [*Aside*]‡
Oh lord, what does he say? Am I discovered now?

WILLMORE.
Do you see this young spark here?

HELLENA. [*Aside*]‡
He'll tell her who I am.

WILLMORE.
Who do you think this is? 330

HELLENA. [*Aside*]‡
Ay, ay, he does know me —
Nay, dear captain! I am undone if you discover me.

WILLMORE.
Nay, nay, no cogging; she shall know what a precious mistress I
have.

HELLENA.
Will you be such a devil? 335

WILLMORE. [*Aside.*] ‡
Nay, nay, I'll teach you to spoil sport you will not make.
— This small ambassador comes not from a person of quality as
you imagine, and he says, but from a very errant gypsy, the talk-
ingest, pratingest, cantingest little animal thou ever saw'st.

ANGELLICA.
What news you tell me, that's the thing I mean. 340

HELLENA. [*Aside.*]
Would I were well off the place; if ever I go a captain-hunting
again —

WILLMORE.
Mean that thing? That gypsy thing? Thou may'st as well be jealous of thy monkey or parrot, as of her; a German motion were
worth a dozen of her, and a dream were a better enjoyment, a 345
creature of a constitution fitter for heaven than man.

HELLENA. [*Aside.*]
Though I'm sure he lies, yet this vexes me.

---

325 fit] pay back
333 cogging] wheedling, begging
344 motion] puppet

ANGELLICA.

You are mistaken, she's a Spanish woman
Made up of no such dull materials.

WILLMORE.

Materials, egad an thee be made of any that will either dispense   350
or admit of love, I'll be bound to continence.

HELLENA.   [*Aside to him.*]

Unreasonable man, do you think so?

WILLMORE.†

You may return, my little brazen head, and tell your lady that till
she be handsome enough to be beloved, or I dull enough to be
religious, there will be small hopes of me.   355

ANGELLICA.

Did you not promise then to marry her?

WILLMORE.

Not I, by heaven.

ANGELLICA.

You cannot undeceive my fears and torments, till you have
vowed you will not marry her.

HELLENA.   [*Aside.*]

If he swears that, he'll be revenged on me indeed for all my   360
rogueries.

ANGELLICA.

I know what arguments you'll bring up against me — fortune, and
honour —

WILLMORE.

Honour, I tell you, I hate it in your sex, and those that fancy
themselves possessed of that foppery are the most impertinently   365
troublesome of all womankind, and will transgress nine com-
mandments to keep one, and to satisfy your jealousy, I swear.

HELLENA.   [*Aside to him.*]

Oh, no swearing, dear captain.

WILLMORE.

If it were possible I should ever be inclined to marry, it should be
some kind young sinner, one that has generosity enough to give   370
a favour handsomely to one that can ask it discreetly, one that

---

353 brazen head] a brazen (brass) head which can speak or prophesy

has wit enough to manage an intrigue of love — oh, how civil such a wench is, to a man that does her the honour to marry her.

ANGELLICA.

By heaven, there's no faith in anything he says.

Enter Sebastian.

SEBASTIAN.

Madam, Don Antonio —   375

ANGELLICA.

Come hither.

HELLENA.   [*Aside*]‡

Ha! Antonio! He may be coming hither and he'll certainly discover me; I'll therefore retire without a ceremony.

Exit Hellena.

ANGELLICA.

I'll see him; get my coach ready.

SEBASTIAN.

It waits you, madam.   380

WILLMORE.

This is lucky. What, madam, now I may be gone and leave you to the enjoyment of my rival?

ANGELLICA.

Dull man, that can'st not see how ill, how poor,

That false dissimulation looks — begone,

And never let me see thy cozening face again,   385

Lest I relapse and kill thee.

WILLMORE.

Yes, you can spare me now — farewell, till you're in better humour — I'm glad of this release —

[*Aside*]‡ Now for my gypsy:

For though to worse we change, yet still we find   390

New joys, new charms, in a new miss that's kind.

Exit Willmore.

ANGELLICA.

He's gone, and in this ague of my soul,

The shivering fit returns;

Oh, with what willing haste he took his leave,
As if the longed-for minute were arrived   395
Of some blest assignation.
In vain I have consulted all my charms,
In vain this beauty prized, in vain believed
My eyes could kindle any lasting fires.
I had forgot my name, my infamy,   400
And the reproach that honour lays on those
That dare pretend a sober passion here.
Nice reputation, though it leave behind
More virtues than inhabit where that dwells,
Yet that once gone, those virtues shine no more.   405
Then since I am not fit to be beloved,
I am resolved to think on a revenge
On him that soothed me thus to my undoing.

Exeunt.

Scene III: A Street.   IV.iii

Enter Florinda and Valeria in habits different from that
they have been seen in.

FLORINDA.
We're happily escaped, and yet I tremble still.

VALERIA.
Lover, and fear! Why, I am but half an one, and yet I have courage for any attempt. Would Hellena were here, I would fain have
had her as deep in this mischief as we; she'll fare but ill else, I
doubt.   5

FLORINDA.
She pretended a visit to the Augustine nuns, but I believe some
other design carried her out; pray heaven we light on her.
Prithee what did'st do with Callis?

---

7 Augustine nuns] nuns of the order of St. Augustine

VALERIA.

When I saw no reason would do good on her, I followed her into
the wardrobe, and as she was looking for something in a great   10
chest, I toppled her in by the heels, snatched the key of the apartment where you were confined, locked her in, and left her bawl-
ing for help.

FLORINDA.

'Tis well you resolve to follow my fortunes, for thou darest never
appear at home again after such an action.   15

VALERIA.

That's according as the young stranger and I shall agree. But to
our business — I delivered your letter, your note† to Belvile, when
I got out under pretence of going to mass. I found him at his
lodging, and believe me it came seasonably, for never was a man
in so desperate a condition. I told him of your resolution of mak-   20
ing your escape today if your brother would be absent long
enough to permit you; if not, to die rather than be Antonio's.

FLORINDA.

Thou should'st have told him I was confined to my chamber
upon my brother's suspicion that the business on the Molo was a
plot laid between him and I.   25

VALERIA.

I said all this, and told him your brother was now gone to his de-
votions, and he resolves to visit every church till he find him; and
not only undeceive him in that, but caress him so as shall delay
his return home.

FLORINDA.

Oh heavens! He's here, and Belvile with him too.   30

They put on their vizards.

*Enter Don Pedro, Belvile, Willmore; Belvile and Don Pedro seeming in
serious discourse.*

VALERIA.

Walk boldly by them, and I'll come at distance, lest he suspect us.

She walks by them, and looks back on them.

WILLMORE.

Hah! A woman, and of an excellent mien.

PEDRO.

She throws a kind look back on you.

WILLMORE.

Death, 'tis a likely wench, and that kind look shall not be cast
away — I'll follow her.   35

BELVILE.

Prithee do not.

WILLMORE.

Do not; by heavens, to the antipodes with such an invitation.

She goes out, and Willmore follows her.

BELVILE.

'Tis a mad fellow for a wench.

Enter Frederick.

FREDERICK.

Oh colonel, such news!

BELVILE.

Prithee, what?   40

FREDERICK.

News that will make you laugh in spite of fortune.

BELVILE.

What, Blunt has had some damned trick put upon him —
cheated, banged or clapped?

FREDERICK.

Cheated sir, rarely cheated of all but his shirt and drawers. The
unconscionable whore, too, turned him out before consumma-   45
tion, so that traversing the streets at midnight, the watch found
him in this fresco, and conducted him home. By heaven, 'tis such
a sight, and yet I durst as well been hanged as laugh at him or
pity him; he beats all that do but ask him a question, and is in
such an humour.   50

---

38 antipodes] the other side of the earth
43 banged] beaten
43 clapped] hit, struck; also, to get the clap (venereal disease)

PEDRO.

Who is't has met with this ill usage, sir?

BELVILE.

A friend of ours whom you must see for mirth's sake.

[*Aside.*] I'll employ him to give Florinda time for an escape.

PEDRO.

What is he?

BELVILE.

A young countryman of ours, one that has been educated at so   55
plentiful a rate, he yet ne'er knew the want of money, and 'twill
be a great jest to see how simply he'll look without it. For my
part, I'll lend him none, and the rogue know not how to put on a
borrowing face, and ask first; I'll let him see how good 'tis to play
our parts while I play his – prithee Frederick, do you go home   60
and keep him in that posture till we come.

Exeunt.

Enter Florinda from the farther end of the scene, looking behind her.

FLORINDA.

I am followed still – hah – my brother too, advancing this way.
Good heavens, defend me from being seen by him.

She goes off.

Enter Willmore, and after him Valeria, at a little distance.

WILLMORE.

Ah! There she sails; she looks back as she were willing to be
boarded. I'll warrant her prize.   65

He goes out, Valeria following.

Enter Hellena, just as he goes out, with a page.

---

65 sails...boarded...prize] In sea battles and piracy, captured ships, called prizes, were
   seized as the property of those who boarded them.

HELLENA.

Hah, is not that my captain that has a woman in chase? 'Tis not Angellica. Boy, follow those people at a distance, and bring me an account where they go in — I'll find his haunts, and plague him everywhere — ha — my brother —

Exit page; Belvile, Willmore, Pedro cross the stage; Hellena runs off.

Scene IV

Scene changes to another street. Enter Florinda.

FLORINDA.

What shall I do, my brother now pursues me;
Will no kind power protect me from his tyranny?
Hah, here's a door open; I'll venture in, since nothing can be worse than to fall into his hands. My life and honour are at stake, and my necessity has no choice. 5

She goes in.
Enter Valeria and Hellena's page peeping after Florinda.

PAGE.

Here she went in; I shall remember this house.

Exit Boy.

VALERIA.

This is Belvile's lodging; she's gone in as readily as if she knew it — hah — here's that mad fellow again. I dare not venture in — I'll watch my opportunity.

Goes aside.
Enter Willmore, gazing about him.

WILLMORE.

I have lost her hereabouts. Pox on't, she must not scape me so. 10

Goes out.

Scene V

Scene changes to Blunt's chamber; discovers him sitting on a couch in his
shirt and drawers, reading.

BLUNT.

So, now my mind's a little at peace, since I have resolved revenge
— a pox on this tailor though, for not bringing home the clothes I
bespoke; and a pox of all poor cavaliers; a man can never keep a
spare suit for 'em; and I shall have these rogues come in and find
me naked, and then I'm undone. But I'm resolved to arm myself   5
— the rascals shall not insult over me too much.

Puts on an old rusty sword, and buff belt.

Now, how like a morris dancer I am equipped — a fine lady-like
whore to cheat me thus, without affording me a kindness for my
money. A pox light on her, I shall never be reconciled to the sex
more; she has made me as faithless as a physician, as unchari-   10
table as a churchman, and as ill-natured as a poet. Oh, how I'll
use all womankind hereafter! What would I give to have one of
'em within my reach now! Any mortal thing in petticoats, kind
fortune, lend me, and I'll forgive thy last night's malice. Here's a
cursed book too (a warning to all young travellers) that can in-   15
struct me how to prevent such mischiefs now 'tis too late; well,
'tis a rare convenient thing to read a little now and then, as well
as hawk and hunt.

Sits down again and reads.

Enter to him Florinda.

FLORINDA.

This house is haunted sure; 'tis well furnished and no living thing
inhabits it — hah — a man; heavens, how he's attired! Sure 'tis   20

---

7 morris dancer] participant in a traditional English dance performed by men in loose
light clothing, wearing bells and sometimes carrying swords

some rope-dancer, or fencing-master; I tremble now for fear, and yet I must venture now to speak to him. Sir, if I may not interrupt your meditations —

He† starts up and gazes.

BLUNT.

Hah — what's here! Are my wishes granted? And is not that a she creature? 'Sheartlikins, 'tis! What wretched thing art thou — hah!   25

FLORINDA.

Charitable sir, you've told yourself already what I am, a very wretched maid, forced by a strange unlucky accident to seek safety here,

And must be ruined, if you do not grant it.

BLUNT.

Ruined! Is there any ruin so inevitable as that which now threatens thee? Dost thou know, miserable woman, into what den of mischiefs thou art fallen? What abyss of confusion — hah! Dost not see something in my looks that frights thy guilty soul, and makes thee wish to change that shape of woman for any humble animal or devil? For those were safer for thee, and less mischievous.   30 ... 35

FLORINDA.

Alas, what mean you, sir? I must confess, your looks have something in 'em makes me fear, but I beseech you, as you seem a gentleman, pity a harmless virgin that takes your house for sanctuary.   40

BLUNT.

Talk on, talk on, and weep too, till my faith return. Do, flatter me out of my senses again — a harmless virgin with a pox, as much one as t'other, 'sheartlikins. Why, what the devil, can I not be safe in my house for you, not in my chamber, nay, even being naked too cannot secure me; this is an impudence greater than has invaded me yet — come, no resistance.   45

Pulls her rudely.

---

21 rope-dancer] A performer who danced or did acrobatics on a tight rope or slack rope; like a morris dancer or fencing master, a rope-dancer would wear loose, light clothing.

FLORINDA.

Dare you be so cruel?

BLUNT.

Cruel? 'Sheartlikins, as a galley slave, or a Spanish whore. Cruel? Yes; I will kiss and beat thee all over, kiss and see thee all over; thou shalt lie with me too, not that I care for the enjoyment, but to let thee see I have ta'en† deliberated malice to thee, and will be revenged on one whore for the sins of another. I will smile and deceive thee, flatter thee, and beat thee, kiss and swear and lie to thee, embrace thee and rob thee, as she did me; fawn on thee and strip thee stark naked; then hang thee out at my window by the heels, with a paper of scurvy verses fastened to thy breast, in praise of damnable women — come, come along.

FLORINDA.

Alas, sir, must I be sacrificed for the crimes of the most infamous of my sex? I never understood the sins you name.

BLUNT.

Do, persuade the fool you love him, or that one of you can be just or honest; tell me I was not an easy coxcomb, or any strange impossible tale. It will be believed sooner than by false showers or protestations. A generation of damned hypocrites to flatter my very clothes from my back! Dissembling witches! Are these the returns you make an honest gentleman, that trusts, believes, and loves you — but if I be not even with you — come along — or I shall —

Pulls her again.

Enter Frederick.

FREDERICK.

Hah! What's here to do?

BLUNT.

'Sheartlikins, Frederick. I am glad thou art come to be a witness of my dire revenge.

FREDERICK.

What's this, a person of quality too, who is upon the ramble to supply the defects of some grave impotent husband?

BLUNT.

No, this has another pretence; some very unfortunate accident brought her hither, to save a life pursued by I know not who, or

why, and forced to take sanctuary here at Fool's Haven. 'Sheart-   75
likins, to me of all mankind for protection? Is the ass to be ca-
joled again, think ye? No, young one, no prayers or tears shall
mitigate my rage; therefore prepare for both my pleasures of enjoyment and revenge, for I am resolved to make up my loss here
on thy body; I'll take it out in kindness and in beating.   80

FREDERICK.

Now, mistress of mine, what do you think of this?

FLORINDA.

I think he will not – dares not – be so barbarous.

FREDERICK.

Have a care, Blunt, she fetched a deep sigh; she is enamoured
with thy shirt and drawers. She'll strip thee even of that, there are
of her calling such unconscionable baggages, and such dextrous   85
thieves, they'll flay[†] a man and he shall ne'er miss his skin till he
feels the cold. There was a countryman of ours robbed of a row
of teeth whilst he was a-sleeping, which the jilt made him buy
again when he waked – you see, lady, how little reason we have
to trust you.   90

BLUNT.

'Sheartlikins, why this is most abominable.

FLORINDA.

Some such devils there may be, but by all that's holy, I am none
such; I entered here to save a life in danger.

BLUNT.

For no goodness, I'll warrant her.

FREDERICK.

Faith, damsel, you had e'en confessed the plain truth, for we are   95
fellows not to be caught twice in the same trap. Look on that
wreck, a tight vessel when he set out of haven, well trimmed and
laden, and see how a female picaroon of this island of rogues has
shattered him, and canst thou hope for any mercy?

BLUNT.

No, no, gentlewoman, come along; 'sheartlikins, we must be bet-   100
ter acquainted – we'll both lie with her, and then let me alone to
bang her.

FREDERICK.

I'm ready to serve you in matters of revenge that has a double
pleasure in't.

BLUNT.

Well said. You hear, little one, how you are condemned by public   105
vote to the bed within; there's no resisting your destiny, sweetheart.

Pulls her.

FLORINDA.

Stay, sir; I have seen you with Belvile, an English cavalier; for his
sake use me kindly; you know him, sir.

BLUNT.

Belvile, why yes, sweeting, we do know Belvile, and wish he were   110
with us now; he's a cormorant at whore and bacon; he'd have a
limb or two of thee, my virgin pullet, but 'tis no matter, we'll
leave him the bones to pick.

FLORINDA.

Sir, if you have any esteem for that Belvile, I conjure you to treat
me with more gentleness; he'll thank you for the justice.   115

FREDERICK.

Harkee, Blunt, I doubt we are mistaken in this matter.

FLORINDA.

Sir, if you find me not worth Belvile's care, use me as you please,
and that you may think I merit better treatment than you
threaten — pray take this present —

Gives him a ring; he looks on it.

BLUNT.

Hum — a diamond! Why 'tis a wonderful virtue now that lies in   120
this ring, a mollifying virtue; 'sheartlikins, there's more persua-
sive rhetoric in't than all her sex can utter.

FREDERICK.

I begin to suspect something; and 'twould anger us vilely to be
trussed up for a rape upon a maid of quality, when we only believe we ruffle a harlot.   125

---

111 cormorant] marine bird known for its voracious appetite

BLUNT.

Thou art a credulous fellow, but 'sheartlikins I have no faith yet; why my saint prattled as parlously as this does, she gave me a bracelet too, a devil on her, but I sent my man to sell it today for necessaries, and it proved as counterfeit as her vows of love.

FREDERICK.

However, let it reprieve her till we see Belvile.   130

BLUNT.

That's hard, yet I will grant it.

Enter a servant.

SERVANT.

Oh, sir, the colonel is just come in with his new friend and a Spaniard of quality, and talks of having you to dinner with 'em.

BLUNT.

'Sheartlikins, I'm undone — I would not see 'em for the world. Harkee, Frederick, lock up the wench in your chamber.   135

FREDERICK.

Fear nothing, madam; whate'er he threatens, you are safe whilst in my hands.

Exeunt Frederick and Florinda.

BLUNT.

And, sirrah, upon your life, say — I am not at home — or that I'm asleep — or — or anything — away — I'll prevent their coming this way.   140

ACT V.

Scene I. Blunt's Chamber.

*After a great knocking as at his chamber door, enter Blunt softly crossing the
stage, in his shirt and drawers as before.*

Call within.

VOICES.[†]

Ned, Ned Blunt, Ned Blunt.

BLUNT.

The rogues are up in arms. 'Sheartlikins, this villainous Frederick
has betrayed me; they have heard of my blessed fortune.

Knocking within.

VOICES.[†]

Ned Blunt, Ned, Ned —

BELVILE.   [*Within.*][‡]

Why he's dead, sir, without dispute dead, he has not been seen   5
today; let's break open the door — here — boy —

BLUNT.

Ha, break open the door. 'Sheartlikins, that mad fellow will be as
good as his word.

BELVILE.   [*Within.*][‡]

Boy, bring something to force the door.

A great noise within, at the door again.

BLUNT.

So, now must I speak in my own defence; I'll try what rhetoric   10
will do — hold — hold; what do you mean gentlemen, what do
you mean?

BELVILE.   [*Within.*][‡]

Oh rogue, art alive; prithee open the door and convince us.

BLUNT.

Yes, I am alive gentlemen — but at present a little busy.

BELVILE.   [*Within.*][‡]

How, Blunt grown man of business? Come, come, open and let's   15
see this miracle.

BLUNT.

No, no, no, no, gentlemen, 'tis no great business — but — I am —
at — my devotion — 'sheartlikins, will you not allow a man time to
pray?

BELVILE.   [*Within.*]‡

Turned religious! A greater wonder than the first, therefore open   20
quickly, or we shall unhinge, we shall.

BLUNT.

This won't do — why harkee, colonel, to tell you the plain truth, I
am about a necessary affair of life — I have a wench with me —
you apprehend me? The devil's in't if they be so uncivil as to disturb me now.   25

WILLMORE.   [*Within.*]‡

How, a wench! Nay then, we must enter and partake no resistance — unless it be your lady of quality, and then we'll keep our
distance.

BLUNT.

So, the business is out.

WILLMORE.   [*Within.*]‡

Come, come, lend's more hands to the door — now heave alto-   30
gether — so, well done, my boys —

Breaks open the door.

Enter Belvile, Willmore, Frederick, Pedro and Boy.† *Blunt looks simply, they*
all laugh at him, he lays his hand on his sword, and comes up to Willmore.

BLUNT.

Harkee sir, laugh out your laugh quickly, d'ye hear, and begone.
I shall spoil your sport else, 'sheartlikins sir, I shall — the jest has
been carried on too long. [*Aside.*] Oh — a plague upon my tailor.

WILLMORE.

'Sdeath, how the whore has dressed him. Faith, sir, I'm sorry.   35

BLUNT.

Are you so, sir; keep't to yourself then, sir, I advise you, d'ye
hear, for I can as little endure your pity as his mirth.

Lays his hand on's sword.

BELVILE.

Indeed, Willmore, thou wert a little too rough with Ned Blunt's
mistress. Call a person of quality whore? And one so young, so
handsome, and so eloquent — ha, ha, he.   40

BLUNT.

Harkee sir, you know me, and know I can be angry; have a care —
for, 'sheartlikins, I can fight too — I can, sir — do you mark me —
no more —

BELVILE.

Why so peevish, good Ned; some disappointments I'll warrant —
what? Did the jealous count her husband return just in the nick?   45

BLUNT.

Or the devil sir — d'ye laugh —

They laugh.

Look ye settle me a good sober countenance, and that quickly
too, or you shall know Ned Blunt is not —

BELVILE.

Not everybody, we know that.

BLUNT.

Not an ass to be laughed at, sir.   50

WILLMORE.

Unconscionable sinner, to bring a lover so near his happiness, a
vigorous, passionate lover, and then not only cheat him of his
movables, but his very desires too.†

BELVILE.

Ah! Sir, a mistress is a trifle with Blunt. He'll have a dozen the
next time he looks abroad. His eyes have charms not to be re-   55
sisted; there needs no more than† to expose that taking person to
the view of the fair, and he leads 'em all in triumph.

PEDRO.

Sir, though I'm a stranger to you, I am ashamed at the rudeness
of my nation; and could you learn who did it, would assist you to
make an example of 'em.   60

BLUNT.

Why ay, there's one speaks sense now, and han'somely; and let
me tell you, gentlemen, I should not have showed myself like a
Jack Pudding, thus to have made you mirth, but that I have revenge within my power. For know, I have got into my possession
a female who had better have fallen under any curse than the   65

---

63 Jack Pudding] a clown or buffoon; clowning assistant to a mountebank or street
performer; a merry Andrew.

ruin I design her; 'sheartlikins, she assaulted me here in my own lodgings, and had doubtless committed a rape upon me, had not this sword defended me.

FREDERICK.

I know not that, but o'my[†] conscience, thou had ravished her, had she not redeemed herself with a ring — let's see't, Blunt.   70

Blunt shows the ring.

BELVILE.

[*Aside*] The ring I gave Florinda, when we exchanged[†] our vows — harkee Blunt —

Goes to whisper to him.

WILLMORE.

No whispering, good colonel, there's a woman in the case; no whispering.

BELVILE.

Harkee fool, be advised, and conceal both the ring and the story   75 for your reputation's sake. Do not let people know what despised cullies we English are, to be cheated and abused by one whore, and another rather bribe thee than be kind to thee is an infamy to our nation.

WILLMORE.

Come, come, where's the wench? We'll see her, let her be what   80 she will; we'll see her.

PEDRO.

Ay, ay, let us see her. I can soon discover whether she be of quality, or for your diversion.

BLUNT.

She's in Fred's custody.

WILLMORE.

Come, come, the key.   85

To Frederick who gives him the key; they are going.

BELVILE.

Death, what shall I do — Stay gentlemen — yet if I hinder 'em, I
shall discover all — hold — let's go at once — give me the key.

WILLMORE.

Nay, hold there colonel; I'll go first.

FREDERICK.

Nay, no dispute; Ned and I have the propriety of her.

WILLMORE.

Damn propriety — then we'll draw cuts — [*Belvile goes to whisper to
Willmore.*] nay, no corruption, good colonel. Come, the longest
sword carries her —

They all draw, forgetting Don Pedro, being as a Spaniard, had the longest.

BLUNT.

I yield up my interest to you, gentlemen, and that will be revenge
sufficient.

WILLMORE. [*To Pedro.*]

The wench is yours —

[*Aside.*] Pox of his Toledo; I had forgot that.

FREDERICK.

Come sir, I'll conduct you to the lady.

Exeunt Frederick and Pedro.

BELVILE. [*Aside.*]

To hinder him will certainly discover her —
— Dost know, dull beast, what mischief thou hast done?

Willmore walking up and down out of humour.

WILLMORE.

Ay, ay, to trust our fortune to lots, a devil on't; 'twas madness,
that's the truth on't.

BELVILE.

Oh intolerable sot —

Stage Direction: longest] reference to a Spanish fashion for long swords
96 Toledo] sword made in Toledo, famous for its fine steel

Enter Florinda running masked, Pedro after her;
Willmore gazing round her.

FLORINDA. [*Aside.*]
Good heaven, defend me from discovery.

PEDRO.
'Tis but in vain to fly me, you're fallen to my lot.

BELVILE.
Sure she's undiscovered yet, but now I fear there is no way to   105
bring her off.

WILLMORE.
Why, what a pox; is not this my woman, the same I followed but
now?

Pedro talking to Florinda, who walks up and down.

PEDRO.
As if I did not know ye, and your business here.

FLORINDA. [*Aside.*]
Good heaven, I fear he does indeed –   110

PEDRO.
Come, pray be kind; I know you meant to be so when you entered here, for these are proper gentlemen.

WILLMORE.
But sir – perhaps the lady will not be imposed upon. She'll
choose her man.

PEDRO.
I am better bred, than† not to leave her choice free.   115

Enter Valeria, and is surprised at sight of Don Pedro.

VALERIA. [*Aside.*]
Don Pedro here! There's no avoiding him.

FLORINDA. [*Aside.*]
Valeria! Then I'm undone –

VALERIA.
Oh! Have I found you, sir –

To Pedro, running to him.

– the strangest accident – if I had breath – to tell it.

PEDRO.

Speak — is Florinda safe? Hellena well?   120

VALERIA.

Ay, ay sir — Florinda — is safe — from any fears of you.

PEDRO.

Why, where's Florinda? Speak —

VALERIA.

Ay, where indeed sir, I wish I could inform you — but to hold you
no longer in doubt —

FLORINDA.   [*Aside.*]

Oh, what will she say —   125

VALERIA.

She's fled away in the habit — of one of her pages, sir — but Callis
thinks you may retrieve her yet. If you make haste away, she'll tell
you, sir, the rest — [*Aside.*] if you can find her out.

PEDRO.

Dishonourable girl, she has undone my aim. Sir — you see my necessity of leaving you, and hope you'll pardon it; my sister, I   130
know, will make her flight to you; and if she do, I shall expect she
should be rendered back.

BELVILE.

I shall consult my love and honour, sir.

Exit Pedro.

FLORINDA.   [*To Valeria.*]

My dear preserver, let me embrace thee.

WILLMORE.

What the devil's all this?   135

BLUNT.

Mystery by this light.

VALERIA.

Come, come, make haste and get yourselves married quickly, for
your brother will return again.

BELVILE.

I'm so surprised with fears and joys, so amazed to find you her in
safety, I can scarce persuade my heart into a faith of what I see.   140

WILLMORE.

Harkee colonel, is this that mistress who has cost you so many
sighs, and me so many quarrels with you?

BELVILE.

It is — [*To Florinda*] Pray give him the honour of your hand.

WILLMORE.

Thus it must be received then.

Kneels and kisses her hand.

And with it give your pardon, too.   145

FLORINDA.

The friend to Belvile may command me anything.

WILLMORE.   [*Aside.*]

Death, would I might; 'tis a surprising beauty.

BELVILE.

Boy, run and fetch a father instantly.

Exit Boy.

FREDERICK.

So, now do I stand like a dog, and have not a syllable to plead my
own cause with; by this hand, madam, I was never thoroughly   150
confounded before, nor shall I ever more dare look up with confidence, till you are pleased to pardon me.

FLORINDA.

Sir, I'll be reconciled to you on one condition, that you'll follow
the example of your friend, in marrying a maid that does not
hate you, and whose fortune (I believe) will not be unwelcome to   155
you.

FREDERICK.

Madam, had I no inclinations that way, I should obey your kind
commands.

BELVILE.

Who, Frederick marry? He has so few inclinations for womankind, that had he been possessed of paradise he might have con-   160
tinued there to this day, if no crime but love could have disinher-
ited him.

FREDERICK.

Oh, I do not use to boast of my intrigues.

BELVILE.

Boast, why thou dost nothing but boast; and I dare swear, wert
thou as innocent from the sin of the grape, as thou art from the   165

apple, thou might'st yet claim that right in Eden which our first
parents lost by too much loving.

FREDERICK.

I wish this lady would think me so modest a man.

VALERIA.

She would be sorry then, and not like you half as well, and I
should be loath to break my word with you, which was, that if   170
your friend and mine agreed, it should be a match between you
and I.

She gives him her hand.

saves
the day.

FREDERICK.

Bear witness, colonel, 'tis a bargain.

Kisses her hand.

BLUNT.   [*To Florinda.*]

I have a pardon to beg too, but 'sheartlikins, I am so out of countenance that I'm a dog if I can say anything to purpose.   175

FLORINDA.

Sir, I heartily forgive you all.

BLUNT.

That's nobly said, sweet lady — Belvile, prithee present her her
ring again; for I find I have not courage to approach her myself.

Gives him the ring; he gives it† to Florinda.

Enter Boy.

BOY.

Sir, I have brought the father that you sent for.

BELVILE.

'Tis well, and now my dear Florinda, let's fly to complete that   180
mighty joy we have so long wished and sighed for. Come
Frederick — you'll follow?

FREDERICK.

Your example, sir, 'twas ever my ambition in war, and must be so
in love.

WILLMORE.

And must not I see this juggling knot tied?   185

BELVILE.

No, thou shalt do us better service, and be our guard, lest Don Pedro's sudden return interrupt the ceremony.

WILLMORE.

Content — I'll secure this pass.

Exeunt Belvile, Florinda, Frederick and Valeria.

Enter Boy.

BOY. [*To Willmore.*]

Sir, there's a lady without would speak to you.

WILLMORE.

Conduct her in, I dare not quit my post.   190

BOY.

And sir, your tailor waits you in your chamber.

BLUNT.

Some comfort yet, I shall not dance naked at the wedding.

Exeunt Blunt and Boy.

*Enter again the Boy, conducting in
Angellica in a masquing habit and a vizard. Willmore runs to her.*

WILLMORE.

This can be none but my pretty gypsy — oh, I see you can follow as well as fly. Come, confess thyself the most malicious devil in nature; you think you have done my business with Angellica —   195

ANGELLICA.

Stand off, base villain —

She draws a pistol, and holds it to his breast.

WILLMORE.

Hah, 'tis not she; who art thou? And what's thy business?

ANGELLICA.

One thou hast injured, and who comes to kill thee for't.

WILLMORE.

What the devil canst thou mean?

ANGELLICA.

By all my hopes to kill thee —   200

Holds still the pistol to his breast, he going back, she following still.

WILLMORE.
  Prithee, on what acquaintance? For I know thee not.
ANGELLICA.
  Behold this face — so lost to thy remembrance,
  And then call all thy sins about thy soul,

Pulls off her vizard.

  And let 'em die with thee.
WILLMORE.
  Angellica!   205
ANGELLICA.
  Yes, traitor,†
  Does not thy guilty blood run shivering through thy veins?
  Hast thou no horror at this sight that tells thee
  Thou hast not long to boast thy shameful conquest?
WILLMORE.
  Faith, no, child; my blood keeps its old ebbs and flows still, and   210
  that usual heat too, that could oblige thee with a kindness, had I
  but opportunity.
ANGELLICA.
  Devil! Dost wanton with my pain — have at thy heart.
WILLMORE.
  Hold, dear virago! Hold thy hand a little; I am not now at leisure
  to be killed — hold and hear me —   215
  [*Aside*] — Death, I think she's in earnest.
ANGELLICA.   [*Aside, turning from him.*]
  Oh, if I take not heed,
  My coward heart will leave me to his mercy.
    — What have you, sir, to say? But should I hear thee,
  Thou'dst talk away all that is brave about me: 220

Follows him with the pistol to his breast.

  And I have vowed thy death, by all that's sacred.

---

214 virago] strong or angry woman; a female warrior

WILLMORE.

    Why, then there's an end of a proper handsome fellow,

    That might 'a' lived to have done good service yet;

    That's all I can say to't.

ANGELLICA.   [*Pausingly.*]

    Yet — I would give thee — time for — penitence.   225

WILLMORE.

    Faith child, I thank God I have ever took

    Care to lead a good sober, hopeful life, and am of a religion

    That teaches me to believe I shall depart in peace.

ANGELLICA.

    So will the devil! Tell me,

    How many poor believing fools thou hast undone?   230

    How many hearts thou hast betrayed to ruin?

    Yet these are little mischiefs to the ills

    Thou'st taught mine to commit: thou'st taught it love.

WILLMORE.

    Egad, 'twas shrewdly hurt the while.

ANGELLICA.

    Love, that has robbed it of its unconcern   235

    Of all that pride that taught me how to value it.

    And in its room

    A mean submissive passion was conveyed,

    That made me humbly bow, which I ne'er did

    To any thing but heaven.   240

    Thou, perjured man, didst this, and with thy oaths,

    Which on thy knees, thou didst devoutly make,

    Softened my yielding heart — and then, I was a slave —

    Yet still had been content to've worn my chains,

    Worn 'em with vanity and joy for ever,   245

    Hadst thou not broke those vows that put them on.

    'Twas then I was undone.

       All this while follows him with the pistol to his breast.

WILLMORE.

    Broke my vows! Why, where hast thou lived?

    Amongst the gods? For I never heard of mortal man

    That has not broke a thousand vows.   250

ANGELLICA.

    Oh impudence!

WILLMORE.

Angellica! That beauty has been too long tempting
Not to have made a thousand lovers languish,
Who in the amorous fever[†] no doubt have sworn
Like me; did they all die in that faith? Still adoring? 255
I do not think they did.

ANGELLICA.

No, faithless man; had I repaid their vows, as I did thine,
I would have killed the ingrateful that had abandoned me.

WILLMORE.

This old general has quite spoiled thee; nothing makes a woman
so vain as being flattered. Your old lover ever supplies the de- 260
fects of age, with intolerable dotage, vast charge, and that which
you call constancy; and attributing this to your own merits, you
domineer, and throw your favours in's teeth, upbraiding him still
with the defects of age, and cuckold him as often as he deceives
your expectations. But the gay, young, brisk lover that brings his 265
equal fires, and can give you dart for dart, will be[†] as nice as you
sometimes.

ANGELLICA.

All this thou'st made me know, for which I hate thee.
Had I remained in innocent security,
I should have thought all men were born my slaves, 270
And worn my pow'r like lightning in my eyes,
To have destroyed at pleasure when offended.
But when love held the mirror, the undeceiving glass
Reflected all the weakness of my soul, and made me know
My richest treasure being lost, my honour, 275
All the remaining spoil could not be worth
The conqueror's care or value.
Oh how I fell, like a long worshipped idol
Discovering all the cheat.
Would not the incense and rich sacrifice 280
Which blind devotion offered at my altars,
Have fall'n to thee?
Why wouldst thou then destroy my fancied pow'r?

WILLMORE.

By heaven thou'rt brave, and I admire thee strangely.
I wish I were that dull, that constant thing 285
Which thou wouldst have, and nature never meant me.
I must, like cheerful birds, sing in all groves,

                And perch on every bough,
                Billing the next kind she that flies to meet me;
                Yet after all could build my nest with thee,   290
                Thither repairing when I'd loved my round,
                And still reserve a tributary flame.
                To gain your credit, I'll pay you back your charity,
                And be obliged for nothing but for love.

                        Offers her a purse of gold.

ANGELLICA.
                Oh that thou wert in earnest!   295
                So mean a thought of me,
                Would turn my rage to scorn, and I should pity thee,
                And give thee leave to live;
                Which for the public safety of our sex,
                And my own private injuries, I dare not do,   300
                Prepare —

                        Follows still, as before.

                I will no more be tempted with replies.
WILLMORE.
                Sure —
ANGELLICA.
                Another word will damn thee! I've heard thee talk too long.

        She follows him with the pistol ready to shoot; he retires still amazed.

        Enter Don Antonio, his arm in a scarf, and lays hold on the pistol.†

ANTONIO.
                Hah! Angellica!   305
ANGELLICA.
                Antonio! What devil brought thee hither?
ANTONIO.
                Love and curiosity, seeing your coach at door.
                Let me disarm you of this unbecoming instrument of death —

                        Takes away the pistol.

Amongst the number of your slaves, was there not one worthy
the honour to have fought your quarrel?   310
— Who are you sir, that are so very wretched
To merit death from her?

WILLMORE.

One, sir, that could have made a better end of an amorous quarrel without you, than with you.

ANTONIO.

Sure 'tis some rival — hah — the very man took down her picture   315
yesterday — the very same that set on me last night — blest opportunity —

Offers to shoot him.

ANGELLICA.

Hold, you're mistaken sir.

ANTONIO.

By heaven, the very same!
Sir, what pretensions have you to this lady?   320

WILLMORE.

Sir, I do not use to be examined, and am ill at all disputes but
this —

Draws; Antonio offers to shoot.

ANGELLICA.   [*To Willmore.*]

Oh hold! You see he's armed with certain death,
— And you Antonio, I command you hold,
By all the passion you've so lately vowed me.   325

Enter Don Pedro, sees Antonio and stays.

PEDRO.   [*Aside.*]

Hah, Antonio! And Angellica!

ANTONIO.

When I refuse obedience to your will,
May you destroy me with your mortal hate.
By all that's holy I adore you so,
That even my rival, who has charms enough   330
To make him fall a victim to my jealousy
Shall live, nay and have leave to love on still.

[V.i]

PEDRO. [*Aside.*]
    What's this I hear?
ANGELLICA.
    Ah thus! 'Twas thus he talked, and I believed.

Pointing to Willmore.

    Antonio,[†] yesterday,   335
    I'd not have sold my interest in his heart
    For all the sword has won and lost in battle.
    But now to show my utmost of contempt,
    I give thee life — which if thou wouldst preserve,
    Live where my eyes may never see thee more,   340
    Live to undo someone whose soul may prove
    So bravely constant to revenge my love.

Goes out, Antonio follows, but Pedro pulls him back.

PEDRO.
    Antonio — stay.
ANTONIO.
    Don Pedro —
PEDRO.
    What coward fear was that prevented thee   345
    From meeting me this morning on the Molo?
ANTONIO.
    Meet thee?
PEDRO.
    Yes me; I was the man that dared thee to't.
ANTONIO.
    Hast thou so often seen me fight in war,
    To find no better cause to excuse my absence?   350
    I sent my sword and one to do thee right,
    Finding myself uncapable to use a sword.
PEDRO.
    But 'twas Florinda's quarrel we fought,
    And you, to show how little you esteemed her,
    Sent me your rival, giving him your interest.   355
    But I have found the cause of this affront,
    And when I meet you fit for the dispute,
    I'll tell you my resentment.

ANTONIO.

I shall be ready, sir, ere long, to do you reason.

Exit Antonio.

PEDRO.

If I could find Florinda now whilst my anger's high, I think I   360
should be kind, and give her to Belvile in revenge.

WILLMORE.

Faith, sir, I know not what you would do, but I believe the priest
within has been so kind.

PEDRO.

How! My sister married?

WILLMORE.

I hope by this time he† is, and bedded too, or he has not my   365
longings about him.

PEDRO.

Dares he do this! Does he not fear my power?

WILLMORE.

Faith, not at all. If you will go in, and thank him for the favour he
has done your sister, so; if not, sir, my power's greater in this
house than yours. I have a damned surly crew here, that will keep   370
you till the next tide, and then clap you on board for prize;† my
ship lies but a league off the Molo, and we shall show your don-
ship a damned tramontana rover's trick.

Enter Belvile.

BELVILE.

This rogue's in some new mischief — hah, Pedro returned!

PEDRO.

Colonel Belvile, I hear you have married my sister?   375

BELVILE.

You have heard the truth then, sir.

PEDRO.

Have I so; then, sir, I wish you joy.

---

373 tramontana] lit., a person from the other side of the mountains; fig., a foreigner,
barbarian

BELVILE.

How!

PEDRO.

By this embrace I do, and I am glad on't.

BELVILE.

Are you in earnest? 380

PEDRO.

By our long friendship and my obligations to thee, I am,
The sudden change I'll give you reasons for anon.
Come lead me to my sister,
That she may know I now approve her choice.

*Exeunt Belvile with Pedro. Willmore goes to follow them. Enter Hellena as
before in boy's clothes, and pulls him back.*

WILLMORE.

Ha! My gypsy — now a thousand blessings on thee for this kind- 385
ness. Egad child, I was e'en in despair of ever seeing thee again;
my friends are all provided for within, each man his kind woman.

HELLENA.

Ha! I thought they had served me some such trick!

WILLMORE.

And I was e'en resolved to go aboard, and condemn myself to
my lone cabin, and the thoughts of thee. 390

HELLENA.

And could you have left me behind, would you have been so ill
natured?

WILLMORE.

Why, 'twould have broke my heart, child — but since we are met
again, I defy foul weather to part us.

HELLENA.

And would you be a faithful friend now, if a maid should trust 395
you?

WILLMORE.

For a friend I cannot promise; thou art of a form so excellent, a
face and humour too good for cold dull friendship. I am parlously afraid of being in love, child, and you have not forgot how
severely you have used me? 400

HELLENA.

That's all one; such usage you must still look for, to find out all
your haunts, to rail at you to all that love you, till I have made

you love only me in your own defence, because nobody else will love you.†

WILLMORE.

But hast thou no better quality to recommend thyself by?   405

HELLENA.

Faith, none, captain — why, 'twill be the greater charity to take me for thy mistress. I am alone, child, a kind of orphan lover, and why I should die a maid, and in a captain's hands too, I do not understand.

WILLMORE.

Egad, I was never clawed away with broadsides from any female   410
before. Thou hast one virtue I adore, good nature. I hate a coy demure mistress, she's as troublesome as a colt; I'll break none. No, give me a mad mistress when mewed, and in flying, one† I dare trust upon the wing, that whilst she's kind will come to the lure.   415

HELLENA.

Nay, as kind as you will, good captain, whilst it lasts, but let's lose no time.

WILLMORE.

My time's as precious to me as thine can be; therefore dear creature, since we are so well agreed, let's retire to my chamber, and if ever thou wert treated with such savoury love! Come — my   420
bed's prepared for such a guest, all clean and sweet as thy fair self. I love to steal a dish and a bottle with a friend, and hate long graces — come let's retire and fall to.†

HELLENA.

'Tis but getting my consent, and the business is soon done. Let but old gaffer Hymen and his priest say amen to't, and I dare lay   425
my mother's daughter by as proper a fellow as your father's son, without fear or blushing.

---

410 broadside] a single sheet of paper printed on one side. Ballads were customarily published on broadsides; Hellena's references to an orphan lover and a captain are characteristic of ballad themes.

413 mewed] of hawks, confined in a cage. Willmore's speech makes several references to hawking, in which a hawk is sent to hunt other birds, and encouraged to return by a lure.

425 gaffer] old man

425 Hymen] god of marriage

WILLMORE.

Hold, hold, no bug words, child; priest and Hymen? Prithee add
a hangman to 'em to make up the consort — no, no, we'll have no
vows but love, child, nor witness but the lover; the kind deity en-   430
joins† naught but love and enjoy! Hymen and priest wait still
upon portion, and jointure; love and beauty have their own cere-
monies. Marriage is as certain a bane to love as lending money is
to friendship. I'll neither ask nor give a vow — though I could be
content to turn gypsy, and become a left-handed bridegroom to   435
have the pleasure of working that great miracle of making a maid
a mother, if you durst venture; 'tis upse. gypsy that, and if I miss,
I'll lose my labour.

HELLENA.

And if you do not lose, what shall I get? A cradle full of noise and
mischief, with a pack of repentance at my back? Can you teach   440
me to weave incle to pass my time with? 'Tis upse gypsy that too.

WILLMORE.

I can teach thee to weave a true love's knot better.

HELLENA.

So can my dog.

WILLMORE.

Well, I see we are both upon our guards, and I see there's no way
to conquer good nature, but by yielding — here — give me thy   445
hand — one kiss and I am thine —

HELLENA.

One kiss! How like my page he speaks; I am resolved you shall
have none, for asking such a sneaking sum. He that will be satis-
fied with one kiss, will never die of that longing. Good friend single kiss, is all your talking come to this? A kiss, a caudle! Farewell   450
captain single kiss.

---

428 bug words] frightening words; related to "bogey"
432 portion and jointure] financial arrangements made as part of a marriage agreement;
portion — money a woman brings to her husband in marriage; jointure — provision
for support of a wife after husband's death
435 left-handed bridegroom] without a legal marriage
437 upse] in the manner or fashion of
441 incle] linen thread, used to weave tape
442 true love's knot] an elaborate knot symbolizing love.
450 caudle] gruel for invalid

Going out; he stays her.

WILLMORE.

Nay, if we part so, let me die like a bird upon a bough, at the sheriff's charge. By heaven, both the Indies shall not buy thee from me. I adore thy humour and will marry thee, and we are so of one humour, it must be a bargain — give me thy hand —   455

Kisses her hand.

And now let the blind ones (love and fortune) do their worst.

HELLENA.

Why, god-a-mercy, captain!

WILLMORE.

But harkee — the bargain is now made; but is it not fit we should know each other's names, that when we have reason to curse one another hereafter (and people ask me who 'tis I give to the devil)   460
I may at least be able to tell what family you came of.

HELLENA.

Good reason, captain; and where I have cause (as I doubt not but I shall have plentiful) that I may know at whom to throw my — blessings — I beseech ye your name.

WILLMORE.

I am called Robert the Constant.   465

HELLENA.

A very fine name; pray was it your falconer or butler that chris-tened you? Do they not use to whistle when they call you?

WILLMORE.

I hope you have a better, that a man may name without crossing himself; you are merry with mine.

HELLENA.

I am called Hellena the Inconstant.   470

Enter Pedro, Belvile, Florinda, Frederick, Valeria.

---

456 blind ones, (love and fortune)] In art, both Cupid, god of love, and Lady Fortune are depicted blindfolded.
466 falconer] keeper of hawks

PEDRO.

    Hah! Hellena!   470

FLORINDA.

    Hellena!

HELLENA.

    The very same — hah, my brother! Now captain, show your love
and courage; stand to your arms, and defend me bravely, or I am
lost for ever.   475

PEDRO.

    What's this I hear! False girl, how came you hither and what's
your business? Speak.

Goes roughly to her.

WILLMORE.

    Hold off sir, you have leave to parley only.

Puts himself between.

HELLENA.

    I had e'en as good tell it, as you guess it; faith, brother, my busi-
ness is the same with all living creatures of my age, to love, and   480
be beloved, and here's the man.

PEDRO.

    Perfidious maid, hast thou deceived me too? Deceived thy self
and heaven?

HELLENA.

    'Tis time enough to make my peace with that. Be you but kind;
let me alone with heaven.   485

PEDRO.

    Belvile, I did not expect this false play from you; was't not
enough you'd gain Florinda (which I pardoned) but your lewd
friends too must be enriched with the spoils of a noble family?

BELVILE.

    Faith sir, I am as much surprised at this as you can be. Yet sir, my
friends are gentlemen, and ought to be esteemed for their mis-   490

fortunes, since they have the glory to suffer with the best of men and kings; 'tis true, he's a rover of fortune, yet a prince aboard his little wooden world.

PEDRO.

What's this to the maintenance of a woman of her birth and qual- 495
ity?

WILLMORE.

Faith, sir, I can boast of nothing but a sword which does me right where'er I come, and has defended a worse cause than a woman's; and since I loved her before I either knew her birth or name, I must pursue my resolution, and marry her.

PEDRO.

And is all your holy intent of becoming a nun debauched into a 500
desire of man?

HELLENA.

Why — I have considered the matter, brother, and find the three hundred thousand crowns my uncle left me (and you cannot keep from me) will be better laid out in love than in religion, and turn to as good an account. Let most voices carry it, for heaven 505
or the captain?

ALL CRY.

A captain! A captain!

HELLENA.

Look ye sir, 'tis a clear case.

PEDRO. [*Aside.*]

Oh I am mad — if I refuse, my life's in danger —
— Come — there's one motive induces me — take her — I shall 510
now be free from fears of her honour; guard it you now, if you can; I have been a slave to't long enough.

Gives her to him.

---

491 the best of men and kings] the future Charles II
503 three hundred thousand crowns] There is some inconsistency about the size of
     Hellena's dowry. Earlier, Angellica tells Willmore that Hellena has two hundred
     thousand crowns.

WILLMORE.

Faith sir, I am of a nation that are of opinion a woman's honour is not worth guarding when she has a mind to part with it.

HELLENA.

Well said, captain.   515

PEDRO.   [*To Valeria.*]

This was your plot, mistress, but I hope you have married one that will revenge my quarrel to you —

VALERIA.

There's no altering destiny, sir.

PEDRO.

Sooner than a woman's will; therefore I forgive you all — and wish you may get my father's pardon as easily, which I fear.   520

Enter Blunt dressed in a Spanish habit, looking very ridiculously;
his man adjusting his band.

MAN.

'Tis very well, sir —

BLUNT.

Well sir, 'sheartlikins, I tell you 'tis damnable ill, sir — a Spanish habit, good lord! Could the devil and my tailor devise no other punishment for me, but the mode of a nation I abominate?

BELVILE.

What's the matter, Ned?   525

BLUNT.

Pray view me round, and judge —

Turns round.

BELVILE.

I must confess thou art a kind of an odd figure.

BLUNT.

In a Spanish habit with a vengeance! I had rather be in the inquisition for Judaism, than in this doublet and breeches; a pillory were an easy collar to this, three handfuls high; and these shoes   530
too, are worse than the stocks, with the sole an inch shorter than

Stage Direction: band] neckband

my foot. In fine, gentlemen, methinks I look altogether like a bag
of bays stuffed full of fool's flesh.

BELVILE.

Methinks 'tis well, and makes thee look e'n cavalier; come, sir,
settle your face, and salute our friends. Lady —   535

BLUNT.

Ha! Say'st thou so my little rover —

To Hellena.

Lady — (if you be one), give me leave to kiss your hand, and tell
you, 'sheartlikins, for all I look so, I am your humble servant — a
pox of my Spanish habit.

Music is heard to play. Enter Boy.

WILLMORE.

Hark — what's this?   540

BOY.

Sir, as the custom is, the gay people in masquerade who make
every man's house their own are coming up.

*Enter several men and women in masquing habits with music; they put
themselves in order and dance.*

BLUNT.   [*To the masquers.*]†

'Sheartlikins, would 'twere lawful to pull off their false faces, that
I might see if my doxy were not among'st 'em.

BELVILE.

Ladies and gentlemen, since you are come so *a propos*, you must   545
take a small collation with us.

WILLMORE.

Whilst we'll to the good man within, who stays to give us a cast of
his office.

To Hellena.

---

533 bag of bays] (?) a bag of bay leaves used in cooking (Link); Kemble amends to "bag of
baize," a thick green cloth.

— Have you no trembling at the near approach?

HELLENA.

No more than you have in an engagement or a tempest.   550

WILLMORE.

Egad thou'rt a brave girl, and I admire thy love and courage.

Lead on, no other dangers they can dread,

Who venture in the storms o'th' marriage bed.

Exeunt.

THE END.

EPILOGUE

The banished cavaliers! A roving blade!
A Popish carnival! A masquerade!
The devil's in't if this will please the nation,
In these our blessed times of reformation,   5
When conventicling is so much in fashion.
And yet —
That mutinous tribe less factions do beget,
Than your continual differing in wit;
Your judgement's (as your passion's) a disease: 10
Nor muse nor miss your appetite can please;
You're grown as nice as queasy consciences,
Whose each convulsion, when the spirit moves,
Damns every thing that maggot disapproves.
With canting rule you would the stage refine,   15
And to dull method all our sense confine.
With th' insolence of commonwealths you rule,
Where each gay fop, and politic grave fool
On monarch wit impose, without control.
As for the last, who seldom sees a play,   20
Unless it be the old Blackfriars. way,
Shaking his empty noddle o'er bamboo,
He cries, "Good faith, these plays will never do.
Ah, sir, in my young days, what lofty wit,
What high strained scenes of fighting there were writ: 25
These are slight airy toys. But tell me, pray,
What has the House of Commons done today?"
Then shows his politics, to let you see,
Of state affairs he'll judge as notably,
As he can do of wit and poetry.

---

1 blade] swordsman; energetic young man
5 conventicling] participating in a religious conventicle, a clandestine meeting of religious
    nonconformists or Dissenters. The "Epilogue" includes a number of references to
    religious groups' disapproval of the theatre on moral grounds.
13 maggot] a whim
20 Blackfriars] a private theatre popular in the early seventeenth century, but closed in
    1642; a style of acting and drama considered old-fashioned in 1677
21 bamboo] a cane

The younger sparks, who hither do resort,   30
Cry,
"Pox o' your gentle† things, give us more sport;
Damn me, I'm sure 'twill never please the court."
Such fops are never pleased unless the play
Be stuffed with fools as brisk and dull as they.   35
Such might the half-crown spare, and in a glass
At home behold a more accomplished ass,
Where they may set their cravats, wigs and faces,
And practice all their buffoonry grimaces.†
See how this huff becomes, this damny, stare —   40
Which they at home may act, because they dare,
But — must with prudent caution do elsewhere.
Oh that our Nokes, or Tony Lee, could show
A fop but half so much to th'life as you.

---

30 sparks] foppish young men
36 half-crown] a coin worth 2s. 6d.
43 Nokes] James Nokes, comic actor (d. 1696)
43 Tony Lee] Anthony Leigh, comic actor (d. 1692)

Post-Script.†

This play had been sooner in print, but for a report about the town (made by some either very malicious or very ignorant) that 'twas *Thomaso* altered, which made the booksellers fear some trouble from the proprietor of that admirable play, which indeed has wit enough to stock a poet, and is not to be pieced or mended by any but the excellent author himself. That I have stolen some hints from it, may be a proof that I valued it more than to pretend to alter it, had I had the dexterity of some poets, who are not more expert in stealing than in the art of concealing, and who even that way outdo the Spartan boys. I might have appropriated all to myself, but I, vainly proud of my judgment, hang out the sign of Angellica (the only stolen object) to give notice where a great part of the wit dwelt; though if the Play of the Novella were as well worth remembering as *Thomaso*, they might (bating the name) have as well said, I took it from thence. I will only say the plot and business (not to boast on't) is my own; as for the words and characters, I leave the reader to judge and compare 'em with *Thomaso*, to whom I recommend the great entertainment of reading it, though had this succeeded ill, I should have had no need of imploring that justice from the critics who are naturally so kind to any that pretend to usurp their dominion, especially of our sex,† they would doubtless have give me the whole honour on't. Therefore I will only say in English what the famous Virgil does in Latin; I made verses, and others have the fame.

FINIS.

5

10

15

20

25

---

3 *Thomaso*] play by Thomas Killigrew. See discussion of sources in "Introduction."
5 pieced] patched
13 Play of the Novella] Richard Brome's *The Novella*. See discussion of sources in "Introduction."

Textual Notes

The copytext is the first edition (Q1). The textual notes indicate the cases in which I have incorporated a reading from an edition other than the first edition. The source of the reading adopted in the text is entered first, followed by sources of variant readings.

The early editions which have been collated for this edition are listed below:

Q1   [Behn, Mrs. A]. *The Rover or, The Banish't Cavaliers*. London: John Amery, 1677. (First edition; quarto). Q1 exists in three issues; only the third issue names Behn (see "A Note on the Text"). I have collated copies from the British Library (BL), Thomas Fisher Rare Books Library, University of Toronto (Fisher), and a microfilm of a copy held by the Huntington Library (Huntington).

Q2   Behn, Mrs. Ann. *The Rover; or, The Banish't Cavaliers*. London: Richard Wellington, MDCXVII [1697]. (Second quarto)

Q3   [Behn, Aphra]. *The Rover, or the Banish'd Cavaliers*. London: Richard Wellington 1709. (Third quarto)

A   *Plays Written by the Late Ingenious Mrs. Behn, Entire in Two Volumes*. London: Tonson and Wellington, MDCCII [1702].

B   Behn, Aphra. *Plays*. 4 vols. London: Mary Poulson, 1724.

I have also consulted the editions by Kemble, Summers and Link listed under "Adaptations and Modern Editions of Behn's Works" in the *Selected Bibliography*.

Speech prefixes and stage directions are found immediately following the line numbers given in the list below.

Prologue

22	correct] Coract Q1
26	gentle] Gentile Q1
42	debauches] Deboches Q1

Actors' Names

1	Jevon] Jevorne Q1.
2	Medbourne] Medburne Q1.
6	Crosby] Crosbie Q1.
7	Blunt] Q2, A, B; Fred. Q1, Q3
11	Percival] Percivall Q1.
17	Diego] *om.* Q1.
19	Boy] *om.* Q1.
21	Barry] Barrer Q1
25	Quin] Gwin Q1. See "Introduction" for a discussion of the confusion between Anne Quin and Nell Gwyn in relation to this role in *The Rover*.
30	Gillow] Gillo Q1.

I.i.45	Pamplona] Pampulona Q1
I.i.64	Colonel] Coll. Q1. All other abbreviations have been silently expanded.
I.i.70	threw] Q3, A,B; through Q1,Q2
I.i.87	a while] awhile Q1
I.i.125	Hotel de Dieu] Hostel de Dieu Q1.
I.i.165	have] Q1,Q3; hate Q2,A,B
I.i.185	Madam] Q3, B; Mad? Q1,Q2,A
I.ii.1	why] The first edition reads "whe", an exclamation used for emphasis or to demand attention; variant of archaic "we" (OED). Since there is no satisfactory modern equivalent for this

now-archaic expression, I have followed the examples of previous editors and changed "whe" to "why" throughout.

I.ii.128	lest] least Q1
I.ii.206	guessed] guest Q1
I.ii.286	geld] gueld Q1
I.ii.313	sale] Sail Q1
II.i.24	BLUNT.] Q3, B; omitted Q1,Q2.
II.i.25	mistress] Mrs. Q1
II.i.26	FREDERICK and speech] runs on from previous line Q1
II.i.27	BLUNT] Q3,A,B; *om.* Q1,Q2.
II.i.33	WILLMORE] Q3; S.P. and speech included in previous line Q1, Q2, A, B.
II.i.34	BLUNT] Q3,A,B; *om.* Q1, Q2.
II.i.81	waist] Waste Q1
II.i.221	a thousand] 1000 Q2,A,B; a 1000 Q1
II.i.226	Hold...fight.] Angellica's line precedes S.D. in Q1,Q2,Q3,A,B.
II.i.267	money] Mo- Q1
II.i.268	FREDERICK] Q3,B; Pedro Q1, Q2, A
II.i.279	Bye] Buy Q1
II.ii.33	pistole] Pistol Q1
II.ii.35	thing] Q3; things Q1,Q2,A,B
II.ii.82	bewitched] Q2, Q3. A, B; bewitch Q1
II.ii.89	though] Q2,Q3,A,B; thou Q1
III.i.7	Loreto] B; Lorreta Q1,Q2,A,B.
III.i.45	would] wou'd Q3; wou't Q1,Q2; won't A,B.
III.i.49	a thousand] Q1 a 1000
III.i.63	not a word] Q2,Q3,A,B; not word Q1.
III.i.78	talk of] Q2, A; talk off Q1, Q3
III.i.83	*Enter Willmore*] Q3; *om.* Q1,Q2,A,B
III.i.84	Ay, ay] I, I Q1
III.i.107	he and she gold] B; the he and the she gold Q3; he and the gold Q1,Q2,Q3
III.i.124	lest] least Q1
III.i.143	barest] Q1,Q2,Q3; bearest A,B
III.i.155	'tis] Q3; 'ts Q1; it's Q2; is't A,B
III.i.214	lose] Q2,Q3,A,B; loose Q1
III.i.221	very fair lady] Q1 (BL, Fisher); very lady Q1 (Huntington)
III.i.278	mistress] Q3,B; Mistris Q2,A; Mrs. Q1
III.iii.15	*shirt, drawers, etc.*] Q1 (BL, Fisher),Q3; shirt, drawers Q1 (Huntington), Q2; shirt and drawers A,B

III.iii.29   dispatched] dispatch Q1

III.iii.45   bowed] bowd Q1

III.iii.49   shore] shoar Q1

III.iv.24   *Exit*] Q3; *om.* Q1,Q2,A,B

III.v.58   pistole] Q2,A; pistol Q1, Q3,B

III.v.65   pistole] pistol Q1

III.vi.30   spiteful] Spightful Q1

III.v.63   ANTONIO] Q3,B; *om.* in Q1,Q2,A

IV.ii.13   I] B; *om.* Q1,Q2,Q3,A.

IV.ii.82   lose] Q3,A,B; loose Q1,Q2

IV.ii.114   lose] Q2,Q3,A,B; loose Q1

IV.ii.127   haste] hast Q1

IV.ii.132   aught] ought Q1

IV.ii.211   above] Q1 adove

IV.ii.229   HELLENA] Q2,Q3,A,B; Angellica Q1

IV.ii.260   he] Q3; she Q1,Q2,A,B.

IV.ii.291   devil] divil Q1.

IV.ii.292   in] Q2,Q3,A,B; *om.* Q1.

IV.ii.300   impudentest] Q3; impudent'st Q2,A;B; impudents Q1.

IV.ii.352   WILLMORE] Q3,A,B; *om.* Q1,Q2

IV.iii.17   your letter, your note] Q1(Fisher, Huntington), Q2,Q3,A,B.; your note Q1(BL).

IV.v.23   *He*] Q3,A,B; She Q1,Q2.

IV.v.51   ta'en] B; tain Q2,A, Q1 (Fisher, Huntington); tame Q1(BL); taken Q3.

IV.v.86   flay] flea Q1.

V.i.1   VOICES] *om.* Q1

V.i.3   VOICES] *om.* Q1

V.i.32   *Boy*] *om.* Q1,Q2,Q3,A,B.

V.i.53   too] to Q1.

V.i.56   than] then Q1.

V.i.69   o'my] Q2,Q3,A,B; O my Q1.

V.i.71   exchanged] Q2,Q3,A,B; exchange Q1.

V.i.114   than] then Q1.

V.i.178   *gives it to*] Q3,A,B; gives to Q1,Q2.

V.i.206   traitor] Q2,Q3,A,B; taylor Q1.

V.i.254   fever] Q3; favour Q1,Q2,A,B.

V.i.266   will be] Q3; you'l will be Q1; he'll be Q2,A,B. Link amends this phrase to "you'll find will be", following an m.s. note in the Luttrell copy of Q1.

V.i.304   S.D.] Q3; follows Antonio's speech Q1,Q2,A,B.

V.i.335   Antonio] Q3; SP (*Antonio*) Q1,Q2,A.

V.i.365   he is] Q1,Q2,Q3; she is A,B.

V.i.371   for prize] Q3; for prise Q1; my prize Q2,A,B.

V.i.404   you] Q3; *om.* Q1,Q2,A,B.

V.i.413   one] Link,Summers; on Q1,Q2,Q3,A,B.

V.i.423   to] B; too Q1,Q2,Q3,A.

V.i.431   enjoins] A,B; enjoin Q1,Q2,Q3.

V.i.546   *masquers*] Q3,A,B; masqueros Q1,Q2.

Epilogue

32   gentle] Q3; gentile Q1, Q2; gentle A,B.

39   grimaces] grimasses Q1.

Postscript

           Postscript.] present only in Q1.

22   especially of our sex] this phrase is not present in the first issue of
           Q1, but is added to some later issues.

Charles Dickens
HARD TIMES
edited by Graham Law

*

Eliza Haywood
LOVE IN EXCESS
edited by David Oakleaf

*

Jane Austen
NORTHANGER ABBEY
edited by Claire Grogan

*

Thomas Hardy
TESS OF THE D'URBERVILLES
edited by Sarah E. Maier

***

Forthcoming in this series

Sara Jeannette Duncan
SET IN AUTHORITY
edited by Germaine Warkentin

*

Anne Plumptre
SOMETHING NEW
edited by Deborah McLeod

Christmas MAGIC

Patricia Hermes

Illustrated by
John Steven Gurney

A
LITTLE APPLE
PAPERBACK

SCHOLASTIC INC.
New York Toronto London Auckland Sydney

ISBN 0-590-50965-9

12 11 10 9 8 7 6 5 4 3 2   6 7 8 9/9 0 1/0

Printed in the U.S.A.   40

First Scholastic printing, November 1996

For Jessica Hermes

Contents

Whose Footprints?

"Obie!" Katie called to her twin brother, Obidiah. "Come here. Look!"

She was standing by the living room window, her face pressed against the glass. "Come see what I see."

"I know," Obie said. He looked up from where he was making paper chains for the Christmas tree. "It's snowing."

"No," Katie said. "I mean, yes. But there's something else, too. Come here and look."

"Okay," Obie said.

He stood up. He stepped carefully over

1

his paper chains and the strings of tree lights that Daddy had left criss-crossed on the rug.

"What?" he said when he got to the window.

"That!" Katie said. The snow was drifting down across the streetlights. It was lying thick on the sidewalks and grass. "In the snow," she said, pointing. "Footprints."

"I don't see any," Obie said.

"There!" Katie said. She put both hands on Obie's head. She turned him so he was looking where she was looking. They looked down the driveway and across the street to their friend Emil's house. Emil lived there with his grandma.

"Oh," Obie said. "I see them."

"Who would be out in the snow and the dark?" she said. "Who walked across our lawn and over to Emil's house?"

Obie shrugged. "Emil, maybe. Or his grandma."

"The footprints are too big for Emil. And his grandma wouldn't go out in the snow," Katie said. "I think it's a mystery guy and we should go figure it out."

Obie shook his head. "Probably just Sam or Matt. I saw them go out before."

"Not," Katie said. "Probably somebody spying on us or on Emil. Let's get our coats on."

She went to the front hall closet. She was singing, " 'It's beginning to look a lot like Christmas.' "

"It is Christmas," Obie said. "Almost."

"I know," Katie said. "But with the snow, now it *looks* like Christmas. And I can smell Mom's cookies. She's been baking all day. And Daddy put up the wreath before he went to the store before. And know what else? Matt and Sam haven't had a fight in a week, and even Baby-Child hasn't been yelling so much."

She had her coat and boots on, and she turned around.

No Obie. He was sitting on the floor again, bent over the paper chain.

"Come on!" Katie said.

Obie shook his head. "Can't," he said.

"I told Daddy I was going to make the longest chain ever. It's going to be a hundred — maybe a thousand feet long."

"I'll help you," Katie said. "After we figure out the mystery."

"Unh-uh," he said.

Katie frowned at him, her fists on her hips. They always did everything together. And they'd been playing spies all week. With Christmas coming, it was a really good time to spy. Especially since she had an idea about those footprints. "How come?" she said.

Obie didn't look up from his chain. "It's dark, kind of," he said.

"Oh," Katie said. She knew Obie was a little scared of the dark. He sometimes thought there were monsters. Nobody else knew but her, and she'd never tell.

"Anyway," he said, looking at his watch, "Mom and Daddy will be mad if you're out in the dark. It's five o'clock."

"In summer, five o'clock is daytime," Katie said.

"It's not summer," Obie said.

"I know!" Katie said. She made a little face. "Okay," she said. "I'll go by myself. I'll be back in a minute. I'll tell you what I see."

She went outside and down the steps, walking carefully so she wouldn't slip in the new snow. It was so quiet out, it seemed like she could even hear the snow falling.

She went across the path to the driveway. She stopped and studied the footprints.

Big ones. Probably a mystery guy — maybe one who was bringing Christmas presents? Maybe that trampoline she and Obie wanted?

She crouched down, wishing she had that magnifying glass she and Obie had had last summer. But they'd lost it.

It was so silent that maybe she could even hear whoever made the footprints. She bent closer to the ground.

No. No snowfall sound. No foot sounds.

She got up and followed the footprints,

from the driveway to the path in the front, then to the tree. The footsteps went around and around the tree.

Why had somebody walked all around their tree?

She wished it had been somebody going to the garage to hide presents, like a trampoline. Mom and Daddy had said no going in the garage until after Christmas, so she was pretty sure that's where they would hide it. Unless Santa was bringing it. Or unless she wasn't getting it.

She looked up at the tree. There were zillions of tiny white lights all over it. She had helped Daddy put them up last Saturday, after they had had their breakfast out together.

Maybe somebody was planning to steal their lights?

Katie frowned. She'd get whoever tried to steal their lights. The tree was beautiful, with the lights sparkling and the snow falling gently.

She stood up just as car lights came sweeping around the curve, heading down the street.

Daddy's car! She could always tell the sound of Daddy's car, the little click-click sound it made. He had gone to the hardware store for fuses for the tree lights and was back already.

She ducked behind the tree, waiting until he pulled into the driveway. When he got out of the car, she'd jump out and yell, "Surprise!" The mystery guy's footprints would have to wait.

She crouched there, waiting. She wasn't afraid in the dark like this, not like Obie. She wasn't afraid of anything. Well, maybe of just one thing. One thing about Christmas worried her. It worried her a lot, especially at night, just before she went to sleep. But it wasn't anything she could talk about.

Thinking about it made a lump come up in her throat, and she swallowed hard.

She started to hum. Humming always made the scary feelings go away.

She pushed her hands down into her pockets. She hummed "Jingle Bells," her favorite.

She hummed really, really loudly.

Big Surprises

At supper that night, Daddy had some big surprises for everyone. The next day they were going to go to the city to see the Christmas tree — that humongous tree that was put up every year. It was about a zillion feet tall. It was decorated with a zillion, trillion lights. Daddy said it was the biggest Christmas tree in the world.

The other surprise was that after they saw the tree, they were going to go to the biggest toy store in the world. And then a third surprise was that on Christmas Eve, the whole family would work at church, bringing food and toys to homeless people.

Katie wasn't too excited about the church part. But she couldn't wait to see the tree and that huge toy store.

When it was time for bed, she was so excited she could hardly sleep. So Daddy brought warm milk up to her and read her two extra stories. By the time he was finished, Katie felt really sleepy.

" 'Night, Toots," Daddy said, using his favorite pet name for her. "See you in the morning."

" 'Night, Daddy," she said.

But when Daddy was gone, Katie wasn't sleepy anymore. She was wide-awake. She couldn't stop thinking about the trip to the city and the Christmas tree and the toy store. Maybe for Christmas, she'd ask for real spy stuff. She also couldn't stop thinking about Santa. And worrying about her big worry.

She sighed and sat up. She looked out the window.

It was still snowing.

She went over to the window. The snow was getting really deep. And there! All around the tree in front — Katie could barely see the footprints. She had forgotten to try and figure them out before. She had had too much fun popping out and scaring Daddy.

For a long while, Katie watched from the window. Maybe she'd see the mystery guy. Or somebody going to the garage.

But nothing moved in the snow, nothing but more snow falling.

Katie went back to bed.

She looked at her clock.

Ten o'clock.

It was very quiet in the house, except for the sound of the TV somewhere downstairs.

She lay back on her pillow. She closed her eyes.

She opened her eyes.

She stared at the ceiling.

She sat up.

"I can't sleep!" she said. She said it out loud.

She picked up Big Bear. "Can you sleep?" she asked him.

She made him shake his head no.

"Me neither," she said.

She held him up to her face.

"Come on," she whispered to him. "Come with me."

She took Big Bear to the window with her.

Together they looked out at the mystery footprints. She frowned. Did they lead to the garage? Maybe. She leaned closer to the window to see better. But she couldn't tell from there.

She squinched up her eyes, but she still couldn't see for sure. Secrets. There were Christmas secrets hidden in the garage. She hoped.

And she was a spy. She and Obie. They should try to figure out the secrets.

"Right, Big Bear?" she said.

Big Bear nodded.

Katie tiptoed over to her closet. She pulled on her snow pants. She pulled on her

snowsuit jacket. Then she put on boots, but she didn't bother with socks.

She looked at Big Bear. "Want to come?" she said.

She made him shake his head no.

She put him down on the bed and tucked him in. Then she tiptoed down the hall to Obie's room. She went over to his bed and bent over.

He was tucked down under his covers, all covered up, head and all. Katie wondered how he could breathe. He always slept that way. Katie knew why, too. It was because it kept away the scary monsters. That's what Obie thought.

"Obie," she whispered. "Wake up."

He didn't move.

Quietly, Katie pulled back the covers. "Obie?" she said.

He just breathed a big breath.

She bent over and blew on his face.

"Stop it," he said. Really loud.

"Hush up!" she said.

She held very still, wondering if Mom

or Daddy had heard. She listened for foot-steps.

Nothing. Just the TV downstairs.

She tried again. "Obie?" she said. She put a finger on his lips to remind him. "Please wake up. We've got to do something."

"What?" Obie said.

He didn't sit up. He didn't open his eyes, either.

"It's important," Katie said.

Obie sighed. He sat up. He opened his eyes.

"What?" he said, super-grumpy. He sounded as mean as a monster.

"Want to go out and spy? See if something's in the garage?" Katie said.

Obie squinched up his eyes. He looked at his little alarm clock. "It's ten o'clock," he said. "After, even."

"I know," Katie said. "Do you want to go or not?"

Obie shook his head. He lay back down. "No," he said.

"But Obie!" Katie said. "We're spies."

"Not for Christmas," Obie said.

"Why not?" Katie said.

Obie didn't answer.

Katie bent over and blew on his face again.

Obie rubbed his face. "Stop it!" he said. "Because you're supposed to be good, that's why. What if Santa saw you?"

He pulled the covers around his neck and turned over. He disappeared into his covers.

Katie made a face at Obie's back. "Silly," she said. "Santa doesn't have a crystal ball, you know!"

She hoped.

Does Santa Know?

Back in her room, Katie sat on her bed and pulled off her boots. She pulled off her coat, then her snow pants.

She dumped them in a heap beside the bed.

She climbed into bed, pulled Big Bear to her, and hugged him close. "Guess what, Big Bear?" she said to him. "I didn't go out in the dark."

She pretended to listen to Big Bear. She pretended he asked her how come.

"Because I'm being good," she said.

She made Big Bear nod his head. Then she thought he said, Santa doesn't have a crystal ball, you know.

"I know," she said. "But just in case."

She snuggled deep into her pillows. Big Bear had a red ribbon around his neck. Katie felt the ribbon, rubbing it back and forth. It was the way she fell asleep.

But she still couldn't sleep. She was worried again with her big worry. Everybody said you had to be good or Santa wouldn't come. Even Obie had just said that. And Katie knew she hadn't been good this year.

She thought of all the things she'd done that weren't good. She'd been mean to Tiffany. She'd bopped her brothers on the head when they took her toys. She and Obie had planned a sort-of Halloween party when Mom was away, even though Mom had said no party this year. Once, Katie had even taken something by mistake — like being a thief, even though she had given it back. And

at school, she had had to sit in the time-out chair about a zillion times.

What if Santa knew about all those things?

What if she didn't get the two things she wanted more than anything else in the world — the trampoline and the tea party set? The tea party set looked just like a tiny castle. When you opened it up, there were all these tea party things inside, including a princess and a dragon to have tea with.

Tiffany had one.

So did Katie's best friend, Amelia.

Katie wanted that and the trampoline more than anything in the world.

But she was thinking about something else, too. At school, Tiffany had said a very bad thing. It was so bad that Katie hadn't told anyone else about it.

But she wondered all the same.

Now she sat up and pushed back the covers. She got ready to go to Obie's room again. She knew he'd be mad, but she had to talk to him about it.

"Come on, Big Bear," she said. "Come with me."

He asked if they were going outside, but Katie said no.

They tiptoed back down the hall to Obie's room.

Katie was quiet.

Big Bear was very, very quiet.

Katie sat down on Obie's bed. He was completely covered up, head and all, keeping the monsters away.

"Obie?" Katie said. "Wake up."

She turned back the covers.

Obie didn't wake up.

She tickled his nose with Big Bear's ribbon.

"Stop it!" Obie said.

"Hush up," Katie said. "Obie, please wake up. I want to tell you something."

Obie sat up. His eyes were still closed.

"What now?" he said.

"Wake up first," Katie said.

"I'm awake," Obie said.

"Promise?" Katie said.

Obie made a little X sign on his pajama top. His eyes were still closed, though.

"Obie?" Katie said. "Know what Tiffany told me?"

"What?" Obie said.

"Tiffany said there is no Santa Claus," Katie said.

Obie opened his eyes. He frowned. "Tiffany's a dummy-head," he said.

"I know," Katie said. "But is she right?"

Obie made a face, that frowning face that he made when he was thinking hard. He shrugged.

"If there's no Santa," Katie said, "who brings the presents?"

"There's a Santa," Obie said.

He looked worried, though.

"I think we should try and find out,"

Katie said. "Do you think anything's in the garage?"

"From Santa, you mean?" Obie said.

Katie shrugged. "Or from Mom and Dad."

"Mom and Dad only give us little presents," Obie said. "Santa brings the big stuff."

"You sure?" Katie said.

"Sure," Obie said. He closed his eyes again. "Now can I go back to sleep?"

He lay down and turned over. He pulled the covers up high around his chin. Then he ducked under and disappeared.

"Obie?" Katie said. "What if there is no Santa? Do you still have to be good?"

"Yes," he said.

"How come?" Katie said.

"Because," Obie said.

And then he began doing his sleep breathing. He breathed deep, deep, deep. He made little puffy sounds from his nose.

Katie could tell that he was already sound asleep.

She sat and listened for another minute. And then she couldn't help telling him her big worry — even though she knew he probably wouldn't hear.

"But what if you're me?" she whispered. "What if you're not good?"

Secret Santa

On Monday, Katie felt happy as she and Obie walked to the bus stop. She knew she had been good in the city yesterday. Very, very good. Maybe Santa had noticed. She'd seen him on the street corner ringing a little bell.

"Obie?" Katie said to him. She swung her backpack around in front of her. "You know about Santa?"

"What about him?" Obie said.

"Well. You're supposed to be good," she said. "Right?"

"I am good," Obie said.

"I know," Katie said. "But does he come to everybody, you think?"

"Yeah," Obie said.

"Bad people, too?" Katie said.

"Really bad?" Obie said.

"Well, maybe sort of bad," Katie said.

"Oh," Obie said. He was quiet a minute. Then he said, "I don't think so. Not to everybody."

Katie frowned. "That's what I think," she said. "And he should. He really, really should. I'm going to write and tell him."

"Don't say anything mean," Obie said.

"I won't!" Katie said.

When they got to school, Katie was still thinking.

A letter. A Santa letter. She wondered if he would answer if she wrote to him. She wondered if he would listen to what she said, that maybe some people couldn't help being bad.

She put away her coat, then went over and looked in on the rabbits in their cage. The class gerbils had run away, and now they had two pet rabbits. The class had named them Ken and Barbie. Katie wondered if the rabbits had been caught in a rabbit trap or something.

Katie turned so that her back was to the room and no one could see. Then she slid the bar out of the little metal ring and quietly opened the cage. She knew she was supposed to ask permission first, but Mrs. Henry, their teacher, was busy counting lunch slips. Besides, Katie knew she'd be careful.

Very carefully, she lifted Ken out. He was all white and fluffy and soft. She held him up against her face. She could feel his little heart beating fast against her hand. It felt like a little motor or something.

He nibbled at her neck. It tickled.

"Hey, Ken," Katie said. "Do you like it here?"

He made little snuffly sounds.

"All right, boys and girls," Mrs. Henry said then. "I want you all to get to your seats, sit up straight and tall, and listen."

Quickly, Katie slid Ken back into his

cage. " 'Bye, Ken," she said to him.

She closed the cage door and slid the bar across it. The bar was supposed to slide into a little metal ring. But the bar stuck. It wouldn't go all the way in the ring. She wiggled it a little. It was still stuck.

"We're waiting, Katie," Mrs. Henry said.

Katie wiggled the bar once more.

The bar still wasn't all the way inside the ring, but almost. It looked tight enough.

Katie hurried to her seat. She sat up on her knees, though, so she could still see Ken and Barbie.

Everybody in class was sitting up straight and tall. Emil Marks stuck his shoulders back like he was in the army.

Katie had never seen Emil do that before. Actually, she had never seen him sit still before.

She wondered how long he could stay like that.

"Everybody ready?" Mrs. Henry said. She was looking at Katie.

Katie unfolded her legs. She sat up straight and tall.

Next to Katie on one side, her friend Amelia sat up straight, too.

On the other side of Katie, Tiffany sat up straight. Her hands were folded on her desk, and her hair was brushed straight back into a ponytail. Even the pencils on her desk were straight. Her back was the straightest of all. Everything about Tiffany was perfect. Except that she was the meanest girl in the class. Perfectly mean.

Katie tried to sit as straight as Tiffany.

It made her back hurt.

"Ouch!" she said.

"Katie, are you listening?" Mrs. Henry said.

Katie felt her ears get hot.

She nodded.

"All right then, boys and girls," Mrs. Henry said. "This is what we are going to do today."

She held up a little box. In it were folded scraps of paper.

"These are your names in here," Mrs. Henry said. "Each person's name is on a slip of paper. I'm going to go up and down the aisle and each of you is to take out a piece of paper — a name. Just take it, but don't look at it yet."

"Why not?" Emil called out. He didn't raise his hand.

Mrs. Henry looked at Emil. She did her wide-eyed look.

Emil raised his hand.

He was always forgetting to do that.

"Yes, Emil?" Mrs. Henry said in her I-want-to-be-friends voice.

"Why can't we look?" Emil said.

"You'll see in a minute," Mrs. Henry said. "This is about being a Secret Santa. And you know what a Secret Santa does?"

"What?" Emil said.

Mrs. Henry smiled. "Each day next week, you bring in a present for the person whose name you get," she said. "And each day you'll get a present because somebody has your name. But it's a secret. You can't tell whose name you have. You'll be a Secret Santa."

"There is no Santa," Tiffany muttered.

Mrs. Henry didn't hear, but Katie did.

Katie made a witch face at Tiffany.

Tiffany pretended not to see.

"I'll tell you more in a minute," Mrs. Henry said. "Just sit still until we each have a name."

She started up and down the aisles.

Amelia, Katie's best friend, smiled at Katie.

"I love secrets!" Amelia whispered.

"Me, too!" Katie whispered back.

Each person picked a name.

When it was Katie's turn, she shuffled all the little slips around.

She smiled up at Mrs. Henry.

Mrs. Henry smiled back.

Katie picked a little folded piece of pa-

per. She held it in her hand while Mrs. Henry went down the aisle. She wondered whose name she had picked.

And then she had a really bad thought. What if she had picked Tiffany? What if she had to be a Secret Santa to perfectly mean Tiffany?

Very carefully, Katie unfolded one end of her paper.

She looked all around her.

No one was looking.

Katie slid the paper under her desk. She laid it on her knee. She unfolded it until it was flat.

She bent to peek at it.

"Mrs. Henry!" Tiffany called out. "Katie's peeking."

"I am not!" Katie said. She crumpled up the paper. She could feel her ears get hot.

"That's enough, Katie and Tiffany," Mrs. Henry said. She didn't turn to look at them.

Katie turned to Tiffany. She made her best witch face.

"Santa saw that!" Tiffany whispered.

"So?" Katie whispered back. "You said there is no Santa."

Tiffany shrugged. She smiled, a mean smile.

"Maybe there isn't," she said. "But maybe there is."

A Season of Magic

"Now, boys and girls," Mrs. Henry said, when each person had picked a name. "Are you ready? You can unfold your paper and read it, but don't let anyone see it."

Katie quickly went to work on hers. It was all crumpled up, and she had to smooth it out flat on her knee. She read it.

"Obie Potts," it said!

Katie looked up at Mrs. Henry and smiled.

Obie! She had gotten her very own brother!

"I got a good one!" she said out loud.

She had forgotten to raise her hand, but Mrs. Henry didn't get mad. She just smiled and put a finger on her lips.

Emil was chewing on his lip, the way he did when he was thinking. He remembered to raise his hand. When Mrs. Henry called on him, he said, "Presents cost a lot." He sounded worried.

Katie thought she knew why. Emil had no mother or father. He lived with his grandma. Katie thought maybe they didn't have too much money.

"But that's the second part of the Secret Santa," Mrs. Henry said, smiling. "You can't spend any money on the presents."

"No money?" Arthur said. "That's silly."

"No money," Mrs. Henry said. "You can make something — like a small drawing, perhaps. Of if your mom is baking cookies, you can bring in a cookie."

"Or a lollipop!" Obie said.

Katie smiled. She knew how Obie loved lollipops.

Mrs. Henry smiled, too. "Yes," she said. "A lollipop would be fine. Or maybe you can bring a used book of your own or a toy, if it's in good condition — and if your mom or dad says it's all right."

"But how come no money?" Arthur said. "I like buying presents. Once I bought my dad some underwear."

Katie started to giggle. Underwear was a silly present.

She looked over at Amelia. Amelia was giggling, too.

Mrs. Henry didn't laugh, though. She just went on. "Well," she said. "Sometimes there's too much attention paid to what we spend at Christmas and at Hanukkah. We can give something that doesn't cost anything. Not anything but love. And that's part of the magic of the season — bringing love and joy to others."

Katie looked down at her paper again. She smiled.

She loved Obie. She couldn't wait to

give him a surprise. But then she wondered how.

She raised her hand. "Mrs. Henry," she said. "If it's a secret, how do we get it to the person?"

Mrs. Henry smiled. "You'll just put the present on my desk with the person's name on it in the morning. And at the end of the day, I'll give out the presents. Nobody will know who they're from."

Katie thought. She had a zillion ideas for Obie. Lollipops. Cookies. A drawing. Maybe she could make a drawing of an airplane — his favorite thing. She could do it on the computer.

But then she had a worry — he knew practically everything about her, all the toys she owned, the computer, everything. If Mom baked cookies and Katie gave one to Obie, he would know who his Secret Santa was.

Katie frowned. Well, she'd figure it out.

She wondered whose Secret Santa Obie was.

She looked all around her. She looked at Ricardo. She hoped Ricardo was her Secret Santa. Ricardo was new in class, and Katie thought maybe she'd like to marry him someday.

"Then," Mrs. Henry said, "on Friday, the last day, we get to tell to whom we've been Secret Santa."

Katie leaned close to Amelia. "I hope Ricardo has me," she whispered.

Amelia nodded. "He's nice," she said. But she was frowning.

"What's the matter?" Katie said.

Amelia was feeling around her hair. "I lost one of my barrettes," she said. "My favorites. There were two."

Katie looked. Amelia was right. There was only one barrette. It was red with diamonds and flowers on it.

"I'll help you look for it later," Katie said. "Who'd you get?"

Amelia made a mad face. "I'm not telling!" she said.

She put a hand over her paper and slid it inside her notebook.

Katie made a mad face back at her.

That meanie Amelia. And she was supposed to be her best friend.

"Girls?" Mrs. Henry said.

Katie looked up. Mrs. Henry was making a mad face, too.

Katie turned back to her desk. She folded her arms.

"So do you all think you understand the rules?" Mrs. Henry said. "Each day next week, you bring in a present. And on Friday, we get to tell who we've been Secret Santa to."

Tiffany had her hand up. She was sitting up straight and tall. She waited until Mrs. Henry called on her.

"Yes, Tiffany?" Mrs. Henry said.

"What if you don't like the person you got?" she said.

Mrs. Henry smiled. "It's a season of magic," she said. "Remember? Maybe some of the magic will be that you'll begin to like that person."

Tiffany shook her head hard. Her long ponytail flew from side to side.

"Unh-uh," she said. "I hate her."

"Oh, it's a 'her,' " Bobby Bork called out. "We know you got a girl, we know you got a girl."

"That's enough, Bobby," Mrs. Henry said.

She turned back to Tiffany.

"I don't think you should use the word 'hate,' Tiffany," she said. "You think about it."

Tiffany took a big breath. She breathed it out of her nose so it sounded like a whistle.

"I won't say it," Tiffany said. She said it very quietly. "But I feel it."

Tiffany looked across to where Katie was sitting. The only person next to Katie

was Irma Wagner. Hardly anybody in class liked Irma. Irma was a big tattletale. But Katie was pretty sure Tiffany wasn't looking at Irma. Tiffany was looking straight at her.

Fighting with Amelia

When Katie got ready for recess that day, she had trouble with her boots.

She sat on the floor in the coat closet, tugging at them.

They were stuck. She could only get her feet partway into them.

She was getting hot from tugging so hard. Her head and hair were hot, and even her back felt sweaty. She pulled off her coat. She pulled off her hat. Then she looked at her feet.

Her socks were all rumpled down from working at the boots so much.

She looked at her boots again.

Maybe she'd been trying to get them on the wrong feet.

She lined the boots up side by side. She made sure the toes pointed in, sort of at each other, because that meant they were the right way.

She tried putting them on again. She started with the left foot and the left boot. But the boot still wouldn't go on. Maybe her feet had grown since this morning?

"Boys and girls?" Mrs. Henry called out. "What's taking so long? I want everyone to line up for recess. Some people are missing. Who's still in the coat closet?"

"I am!" Katie called out. "I'm having trouble with my boots."

"Amelia," Mrs. Henry said, "go help Katie, please."

"It's all right!" Katie said. "I can do it."

She was still a little mad at Amelia for being a meanie before.

But Amelia came into the coat closet anyway.

"It's your socks," Amelia said. "You have to fix them."

"They're already fixed," Katie said.

"Are not," Amelia said. "They're all bunched up. The boots can't fit."

Katie looked down. She pretended to pick fuzz off her socks. But she smoothed the socks out, just a little.

Amelia was watching her, frowning. She looked just like that mean old substitute teacher, Mrs. Morris.

"Stop looking at me," Katie said.

"I'm allowed," Amelia said.

"How come you wouldn't tell me your Secret Santa before?" Katie said.

"Because!" Amelia said.

"Because why?" Katie said.

"Because it's a secret," Amelia said. "Don't you know anything?"

"I know lots of things!" Katie said.

She looked down at her boots. She could feel wet coming up to her eyes. That

Amelia! And she was supposed to be Katie's best friend.

"Hurry!" Amelia said.

"Mrs. Henry said you shouldn't be mean at Christmas," Katie said.

"She did not," Amelia said. "She said you shouldn't hate anybody. Now hurry. Everybody's waiting."

"I'm hurrying!" Katie said.

She smoothed her sock again. She tugged hard on the boot. It slid on.

"See?" Amelia said.

Katie made a face. But she bent and went to work on the other one.

She pulled hard on her sock first.

Her toe came right out through a hole.

Amelia laughed, a silly laugh that sounded like a snake hissing, all noise through her nose.

"Stop laughing!" Katie said. She quickly pulled on her boot and covered the holey sock.

"You have a hole in your sock," Amelia said. "That's silly."

"So?" Katie said. "So do you."

"Do not," Amelia said.

Katie stood up. She pulled her coat on, and then her hat.

She looked at Amelia. "Then how do you get your socks on?" Katie said.

Amelia frowned at her.

"You have to have holes in them," Katie said. "In the top."

Amelia made a face at Katie.

Katie made a mean face back.

"Know what?" Amelia said.

"What?" Katie said.

"Your hat's on backwards," Amelia said. "That's what."

She made that hissing snake sound again.

Katie felt her head.

Her hat *was* on backwards. She could feel the ear flaps dangling practically over her face. She felt dumb.

She just shrugged, though. "I like it this way," she said.

"Silly," Amelia said. "You look silly."

"Ready, boys and girls?" Mrs. Henry said. "Katie? Amelia?"

"Coming!" Katie yelled.

"Really silly," Amelia said.

And then, by accident, Katie's arm swung out. She bopped Amelia really hard, right across her middle.

Amelia stepped back.

She bumped her head on one of the coat hooks that stuck out.

She put a hand to her head.

She let out a yell.

Mrs. Henry was standing in the door-way.

Uh-oh, Katie thought.

"Time-out," Mrs. Henry said.

The Rabbit Is Missing!

The whole next day, Katie had to sit in the time-out chair. It's where bad kids had to sit.

And Katie knew she wasn't a bad kid.

Even though Mrs. Henry thought so sometimes.

And what if Santa thought so, too?

What if there weren't any presents on Christmas morning?

Katie thought and thought.

She figured that Tiffany was probably

her Secret Santa. And even if Tiffany hated her, Tiffany was perfect. Katie thought perfect Tiffany would probably bring perfect presents.

Maybe she'd even bring Katie a tea party castle set.

Katie snuck a look at Tiffany.

She had to stretch forward to do it, since the time-out chair was way in back.

Tiffany was sitting up straight and tall, doing the spelling test. She didn't look as if she was thinking about being a Secret Santa at all. She didn't look like she was worried about the spelling words, either.

Katie sighed and looked at her paper. She was taking the spelling test, too. Everybody was. And she hated spelling.

She looked over at the rabbits in their cage. She couldn't see well from here. She folded her legs under her and rose up, but still couldn't see. She had snuck Ken out again that morning, when no one was looking. He was just the softest rabbit to hold.

But she'd had trouble getting the bar back in place, just like the day before.

"Are you paying attention, Katie?" Mrs. Henry said now.

Katie unfolded her legs. She slid down in her seat and looked at her paper.

"The next word is 'Hanukkah,' " Mrs. Henry said.

Katie sighed. The hardest word in the world.

She frowned at her paper. She chewed on her pencil. She knew you were supposed to sound out a word if you weren't sure of it.

She tried sounding it silently to herself.

Han. A. Ka.

She frowned at it. She wrote it out.

Hanaka.

It didn't look right.

Maybe it was a hard *c* instead of a *k*? She erased the *k* and put in a *c*.

Hanaca.

Katie shrugged. She looked up at Mrs. Henry and waited for the next word.

But Mrs. Henry was looking funny. She was frowning at something.

"Boys and girls," she said. "Did anyone take Barbie or Ken out of their cage?"

Right away, everybody looked at the rabbits' cage.

Katie kneeled in her seat again. Then she stood up.

Barbie, the gray rabbit, was in the cage. The door was a little way open. And Ken, the white rabbit, was not there.

Her fault! She hadn't locked the cage tight.

She could feel her heart thumping hard.

"Ken's gone!" Emil said.

"Yes," Mrs. Henry said. "I noticed."

Mrs. Henry quickly stood up.

She went to the classroom door and closed it tight.

Then she crossed the room and closed the door of the cage. Katie could hear the bar slide across.

"Now, boys and girls," Mrs. Henry said. "I want you to turn your spelling tests facedown on your desks. And then let's look. Everybody. Get under the desks, go in the coat closet, look in the reading corner. He's got to be in here somewhere."

Everybody jumped up and started looking.

Katie slid under the desk. She knew rabbits couldn't climb. She started crawling under all the desks.

"Here, rabbit, here, rabbit," she called softly. "Oh please, oh please, oh please."

She looked all around.

No rabbit.

She crawled on her hands and knees all the way across the room, looking.

Still no Ken. But she met Obie under Tiffany's desk.

He was down on all fours, too.

"Hi, Obie," she said.

"Arf," he said back. He pretended to wag a pretend tail.

Katie sat back on her heels. "Why are you being a dog?" she said.

"Because dogs chase rabbits," Obie said. "Arf, arf."

"Oh," Katie said. "But I don't see any rabbits."

"Me neither," Obie said.

They both looked around.

Half the class was crawling around on the floor.

The other half were in the coat closet. Katie could hear them giggling and talking. It wasn't funny, though. What if Ken had hopped out of the room? What if he had disappeared just like the gerbils had disappeared?

What if it was all her fault?

Tiffany was standing over by the rabbits' cage.

"Mrs. Henry!" she called out. "Katie was playing with the rabbits before. I saw her. Maybe she let Ken out."

Mrs. Henry looked over at Katie. "You didn't take him out of the cage, did you, Katie?" she said.

"No!" Katie said.

She could feel her face get hot. She had taken him out. But she had put him back.

"Are you sure?" Mrs. Henry said.

"Sure, I'm sure!" Katie said.

Her face was burning hot.

"It's all right. I believe you," Mrs. Henry said. She smiled.

Katie didn't smile back. She made a very frowny face.

She was glad, though, that Mrs. Henry believed her.

Even if she hadn't told the truth. Exactly.

Katie looked all around the room.

Everybody was busy looking. Tiffany and Emil Marks were turning over pillows in the reading corner.

Suddenly Katie had a thought.

She knew it was a bad thought. But nobody would know. And it wouldn't hurt Tiffany.

Katie took another quick look around.

No one was looking at her. None of the kids. Not even Mrs. Henry. Mrs. Henry and even Obie had gone to the coat closet.

Very quietly, Katie stood up. She turned over Tiffany's spelling paper.

She looked at the very last word.

Hanukkah.

H-A-N-U-K-K-A-H.

She said it over and over to herself. She knew it was right, because Tiffany did everything right, even spelling.

She put the paper facedown on Tiffany's desk again.

She went over to her desk.

She looked around one more time.

Still nobody looking.

She erased *Hanaca*. She wrote in *Hanukkah*.

She put her paper back on her desk again.

Her heart was pounding hard. But she took a deep breath.

Nobody would know. Nobody at all.

Not even Santa Claus.

She hoped.

Pancakes with Daddy

Katie was about to join the others in the coat closet. But before she could move, something happened very fast.

A fat white rabbit hopped out of the art closet. It hopped right in front of her.

Katie bent over.

The rabbit stopped to sniff at some paint droppings from the easel.

Katie put out her hands.

And Ken hopped right into her arms.

Mrs. Henry was very happy. So was everyone else in class. Katie was happiest of all. Everyone congratulated her on finding

Ken. Even Tiffany said she did good.

Everyone but Amelia.

Amelia just said, "Lucky, that's all." And didn't even look at her.

Then later, on the bus going home, a very bad thing happened. Katie and Amelia always sat in the first seat in the bus, right behind the driver, Mr. Barker. They liked to help him drive the bus, showing him where to stop. They sat together every day going to school, and every day coming home from school.

But since their fight yesterday, Amelia hadn't sat with Katie. Instead, she went straight to the empty seat beside Irma Wagner. She sat down beside Irma. She whispered in Irma's ear.

They both looked up at Katie. Irma giggled.

Katie made a face at them both. Then she went to her usual seat and sat alone.

Every day after was like that. Every day Katie sat alone.

That meanie Amelia. And it had really

been an accident. Well, sort of an accident, the way Katie had hit her.

Finally, though, it was Friday, the last day of the week. And she wouldn't have to see Amelia all weekend. Actually, she didn't care if she didn't see Amelia ever again. And next week was Secret Santa and she'd be getting presents. So who needed old meanie Amelia, anyway?

When Katie got home that day, she sat in her room for a long time, just thinking. Mrs. Henry had said this was a season of magic. She said they were to really think about the magic of love and giving when they were planning their Secret Santa presents.

Katie thought she'd need a *lot* of magic for this Christmas.

First: How could she give Secret Santa presents to her own brother — when he knew everything she did?

Then: How could she keep going to school every single day without a best friend?

And was there really a Santa?

And what if there wasn't?

And the biggest, biggest worry of all: What if you weren't good?

She kept thinking about the rabbit and the cage and about the lie she had told to Mrs. Henry. She thought about the spelling test and that word Hanukkah. It was the only word of all the ten she had gotten right. And she had cheated.

She knew cheating was wrong. But she so much wanted to get some of her spelling right.

Mrs. Henry didn't seem to wonder how come she could spell Hanukkah and nothing else. But Mrs. Henry did say that she'd have to write the wrong words at home ten times each.

Katie didn't care about that. Every week she had to write the spelling words. She stunk at spelling.

But now she had to add cheating, lying, and losing a rabbit to her list of bad things she'd done.

She lay back on her bed and hugged her bear. And she worried.

The next morning was Saturday, the day she and Daddy went out to breakfast all by themselves, without any brothers.

They went to McDonald's, almost always.

That morning at breakfast, Katie was very quiet.

"Something wrong, Toots?" Daddy said, looking at her across the breakfast table.

Katie shook her head.

She pushed her pancakes around her plate.

"Something?" Daddy said.

"Nothing really," Katie said.

"Something special you want for Christmas?" Daddy asked.

Katie nodded. "A trampoline," she said. "And a castle tea party set."

Daddy smiled. "We'll see," he said. "Anything else?"

Katie sighed. "A new best friend," she said.

"Uh-oh," Daddy said.

"We had a fight," Katie said. "Amelia and me."

"You'll make up," Daddy said.

"No, we won't," Katie said. "Amelia has a new best friend. That tattletale Irma Wagner."

"Maybe you could apologize," Daddy said.

"For what?" Katie said. She made her face get very mad-looking.

Daddy shrugged. "Whatever."

"It was her fault," Katie said. Even though she wasn't so sure of that. But Amelia had started it. By not telling about her Secret Santa.

"The season is about love," Daddy said. "Giving and forgiving."

"It's about magic," Katie said. "That's what Mrs. Henry said."

Daddy seemed to be thinking about

that. "I guess," he said. "Because love is magic."

"I don't love Amelia," Katie said.

Daddy just smiled.

They were both quiet while they ate breakfast.

After a while, Katie pushed her pancakes away. They didn't taste as good as they usually did.

"Daddy?" she said. "Do you have to be really good for Santa to come?"

Daddy laughed. "It's a good idea," he said. "At least to try and be good."

"I try," Katie said.

Daddy reached across and patted Katie's hand.

"Of course you do," Daddy said. "You don't have to worry about that. You're a good girl. A very, very good girl."

Katie just looked at him. Then she looked away.

If he only knew.

The Biggest Cookie
in the World

Katie worked that whole weekend on being good. It was hard, but, she decided, not that hard. The hardest part was not fighting with her brothers. But on Saturday, her big brothers, Sam and Matt, played in the yard, snow-tubing, so they didn't bother her much. And Baby-Child was a pain, but he was getting bigger now, so he was kind of fun to play with — when he didn't try to snatch her toys. Besides, she never really fought with him much because he was too little to hit.

And she never, ever fought with Obie. She was being very, very good.

The best part was planning what to do for Obie as his Secret Santa.

She had planned with Daddy, and they had come up with some good plans.

On Monday, Katie was going to give Obie the world's best cookie. She and Daddy had baked them when Obie and Mom went out. They'd gone to pick up Grandma and Great-grandma and bring them over to have dinner.

They made oatmeal cookies, Obie's favorite. Even though everyone in the family would have cookies, it would still be a surprise to Obie because his cookie was different. Katie had made him the biggest cookie in the world.

It was as big as a pancake. She had decorated it with a face. A raisin face. It had two eyes and a nose and the biggest smiling face ever. It even had ears. It looked like this:

Daddy helped Katie wrap it up carefully in plastic wrap and then tissue so it wouldn't get broken. And she put it in a special Christmas bag in her backpack.

She couldn't wait for Monday to come.

After they had finished with the cookies, Katie went to her room and wrote her spelling words, ten times each. All except *Hanukkah*. She didn't have to do that one because she'd gotten it right.

She felt a little guilty again. So, to make up, she wrote *Hanukkah* ten times, too, even though she thought she'd never forget how to spell that word.

By suppertime Saturday night, Katie knew she'd been very, very good. Perfect, even. She thought she was a practically perfect person. She wondered if this was how Tiffany felt.

They all sat down to dinner with Grandma and Great-grandma. Katie loved having Grandma and Great-grandma there to dinner.

Everybody was talking about Christmas. Daddy was talking about the meals and toys they were going to bring to homeless people on Christmas Eve. Sam and Matt both wanted remote-controlled cars, and they talked about them all through dinner.

The cars sounded like such fun that Katie sort of wanted one, too. But whenever she said she wanted what her big brothers wanted, they said she was just a copycat. That made her very mad.

So she didn't say anything about cars.

"And what about you, Katie?" Grandma said when Sam and Matt finally stopped talking cars. "What do you want from Santa Claus?"

"A trampoline," Sam answered, before Katie could even speak.

Katie made a face at him.

"And a castle tea party set," Matt added.

"Will you hush up!" Katie said.

Sam shrugged. "Why?" he said. "It's true. You told us a thousand times already."

"I'm allowed to talk, you know," Katie said. "Besides, there are other things I want, too, and you don't even know."

"What, Katie?" Daddy said. "And boys, Katie's right. Let her answer for herself."

"Girl stuff," Sam said. "She wants girl stuff."

"Nothing wrong with girl stuff," Great-grandma said. She laughed. "So what do you want, my dear?"

Katie looked down at her plate.

What did she want? A trampoline. A castle tea party set.

Something else, too.

She looked up at Daddy. She had told him. But she couldn't say it now. Not in front of her brothers.

A best friend. She wanted a new best friend.

Or an old one who wasn't mean.

But she knew that not even Santa Claus could bring her that.

She looked at her grandmas and shrugged.

"How about a weekend with Grandma and me?" Great-grandma said. "Would that be a nice present?"

"A sleepover?" Katie said.

Great-grandma nodded. "We could do some girl things together," she said.

"Yes!" Katie said. "Like a manicure!"

Grandma nodded. "Sounds good to me," she said.

"And the Discovery Zone?" Katie said. "Could we do that, too? Climb in the tunnels and stuff?"

Great-grandma laughed. "My bones are a little too old for that," she said.

Katie looked at Grandma. "You could take me," she said.

Grandma smiled. "We'll see," she said. "So after Christmas, we'll plan it. A sleep-over."

"Oh, good!" Katie said. "Just girls!"

She made a face across the table at Sam and Matt.

Sam just shrugged. Matt shrugged, too.

Baby-Child banged on his high-chair tray.

Daddy and Mom were smiling.

Katie looked at Obie.

He wasn't smiling.

He was frowning down at his plate. He had that super-mad look that he got some-times. Katie knew he wasn't mad, though.

He always looked like that when he was worried. Or sad.

She thought she knew why.

She took a deep breath. She looked at Grandma. She looked at Great-grandma.

They were looking at Obie, too, worried-like.

Katie looked back at Obie again.

She thought there were tears in his eyes.

"Obie?" she said. "You can come, too. If you want."

Obie didn't look up. He was still frowning but he nodded. "Okay," he said.

Katie looked at Grandma and Great-grandma. "All right if he comes, too?" she said.

They both nodded. They smiled.

"Of course!" Great-grandma said.

"I don't want a manicure," Obie said.

He was still frowning.

"I know!" Katie said.

"That's very nice of you, Katie,"

Grandma said. "To share your time."

It is nice of me, Katie thought. It is. Very nice.

And she hoped very much that Santa Claus was looking.

A Found Barrette

By Sunday night, Katie knew she'd been on her best behavior ever.

She really, really hoped Santa had been noticing.

And by Monday morning, when she and Obie walked to school, she was really excited. She couldn't wait to see how Obie looked when he saw his super-size cookie, his super-size oatmeal cookie with the smiling face.

Katie sang all the way to the bus stop. She sang one of her favorite Christmas songs.

" 'Rudolph, the red-nosed reindeer,' "
she sang, " 'had a very shiny nose.' "

She wiggled her backpack in time to
the music. She turned to Obie. "Come on,
Obie," she said. "Sing."

"No," Obie said. He made a face. "I
don't like that song."

Katie looked at him. "How come?"

He just shrugged. He bent over and
dug in the snow. He picked something up.
"Look at this!" he said.

He held up a little red barrette, dirty
and frozen-looking. It had a flower in the
middle, with diamond-like things all around.
But the diamonds were covered with dirty
snow.

Katie held out her hand. "That's Amelia's," she said. "She lost it last week."

Obie gave her the barrette. She put it
in her pocket.

She'd give it to Amelia. When Amelia
started to be nice again.

She and Obie sat down on the curb to
wait for the bus. They were early, like they

practically always were. Obie hated being late.

"So why don't you like the Rudolph song?" Katie said.

"I feel sorry for him," Obie said. He kicked some snow aside.

"For Rudolph?" Katie said.

Obie nodded.

"How come?" Katie said.

"Because people are mean to him," Obie said. "People call him names and stuff."

"Not people, silly," Katie said. "Reindeer."

"I know," Obie said.

"But then they're nice to him," Katie said. "After."

"It's still mean," Obie said.

Katie shrugged.

She thought about all the times she'd been mean. But mostly, she was nice.

She looked down the block.

Obie was looking, too. He was waiting for his best friend, Arthur.

Katie saw Arthur coming with Bobby

Bork. Behind them, Katie could see Amelia. Usually Amelia came running when she saw Katie.

But not today. And not lately. She still acted mad. And on the bus, she still sat with Irma Wagner. She acted like Katie didn't exist.

Katie began singing again. Who cared about Amelia?

She sang very loud. " 'Rudolph, the red-nosed reindeer . . .' "

Obie got up and ran toward Arthur and Bobby.

They all began circling each other, doing Power Ranger stuff, kicking out at each other like they were fighting.

But it was playing.

Katie thought maybe she'd really like to kick Amelia.

Katie slid a hand inside her coat pocket.

She felt the barrette.

She looked over at Amelia. Amelia had gotten to the corner. She was standing there all alone by the mailbox. She was looking down the block to where Irma Wagner lived. Katie thought maybe she looked sort of lonely.

Katie stood up. Slowly, she walked toward the mailbox. She got sort of near Amelia.

Amelia didn't turn around.

Katie crunched some snow under her feet.

Amelia still didn't turn around.

"Secret," Katie said. She said it pretty loud. "I have a secret."

Amelia turned around then. She looked at Katie.

"Here in my pocket," Katie said. "A secret."

"Everybody's got a secret today!" Amelia said. "Secret Santa."

"Mine's a different secret," Katie said.

Amelia shrugged. She turned and looked away again.

Katie looked, too.

Irma Wagner was coming up the block.

She was dressed in a huge, fat snowsuit. Her mother made her wear so many clothes when it was cold out that she could hardly walk.

Amelia waved at Irma.

Irma tried to wave back. But she was so fat with snow clothes that she could hardly move her arms. They stuck straight out from her sides.

A penguin, Katie thought. Irma looked like a penguin.

Katie looked back at Amelia.

Amelia was dressed fat, too. She looked like a snowman.

Katie smiled.

A penguin and a snowman.

"Hi, Amelia!" Irma said when she got close. "Did you do your Secret Santa?"

Amelia nodded. She moved close to Irma and took her arm.

They whispered together.

Then Amelia turned around. Irma did, too. They both looked over at Katie.

They both laughed.

Katie could feel her ears get hot.

Penguin, she thought. A penguin and a snowman. And I have the snowman's barrette. And I'm *not* giving it back.

She turned away.

The bus was coming and she hurried to be first in line. She'd beat that old Irma and Amelia.

But the boys got there first.

They were already pushing in front of her and up the steps of the bus. Obie was right in front of her, pushing hard.

"Obie!" Katie said, mad-like.

"Sorry!" Obie answered.

But he didn't move out of her way. He climbed the steps with Arthur and Bobby.

Katie gave Obie a hard poke in his back.

He tripped and fell forward on his knees onto the bus steps.

"Whoa there, Katie!" Mr. Barker, the driver, said. "Now you stand back and wait, Katie."

"Me?!" Katie said. "They pushed."

"Just stand back and wait 'til everyone else is on," Mr. Barker said.

Katie could feel tears come to her eyes.

Mr. Barker was supposed to be her friend!

And now she had to wait for that meanie Amelia and Irma.

Katie backed up. She dropped her backpack onto the ground. She folded her arms. She waited while the penguin and snowman pushed ahead of her onto the bus.

And then, after Amelia climbed the steps, Katie grabbed her bag and climbed right up after.

By accident, she stepped on the snowman's heel. One of her boots slid partway off.

"Hey!" Amelia said.

"Sorry!" Katie said. But she wasn't.

Amelia stopped and tugged her boot back on.

Then she and Irma went to their seat together.

Katie climbed up and sat by herself in the seat behind Mr. Barker.

Mr. Barker looked at her in the rearview mirror. "Having a bad day, Katie?" he asked.

Katie glared at him.

Bad day? Terrible day.

Terrible, rotten, awful day. And the day was just beginning.

Smushed-Up Cookie

Things weren't much better when Katie got to school.

The first thing she did was to take Obie's cookie out of her backpack. And when she did, she saw it was all smushed up. The eye part had broken off from the nose and mouth part. The smile part was broken in half. And some of the raisins had fallen off. It had probably happened when she'd dropped her backpack back there at the bus stop.

She laid it on her desk and looked at it. What should she do?

She looked all around.

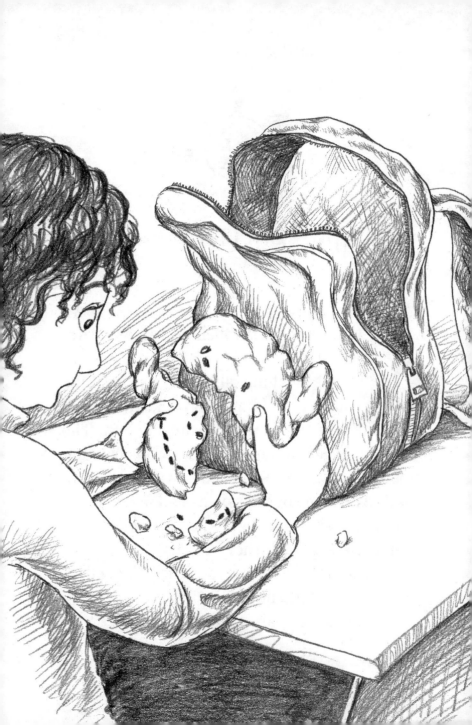

The first ten minutes of class were quiet activity time. Kids were allowed to do anything they wanted, like read or do quiet art projects. They could even talk, if they did it quiet-like.

Katie saw that Amelia and Irma were whispering together on one side of her.

On the other side, Tiffany was bent over, doing something inside her desk.

Other people were going up to Mrs. Henry's desk, carrying Secret Santa presents. Everybody was working on their Secret Santa thing.

Katie looked over at Obie. He was reading, his hands on either side of his head, pressing his ears in. Katie knew that Obie thought his ears were too big, even though they weren't really.

What would he think when he got a smushed-up cookie for a present?

She had to fix it. She bent over her desk and went to work on it. She tried to cover it with one hand while she worked, so that no one would see what a yucky Secret Santa present she had brought. Very carefully, she pushed the eye part down till it met the nose and mouth part.

Bits of cookie crumbled onto the desk.

Katie took a deep breath. She slid the crumbled parts together and pressed her fingers down on the place where they met. She tried to make the parts stick together. Some raisins broke loose and fell out on the desk. Her desk was covered with crumbs and raisins.

Katie made a frowny face. She looked over at Obie again. She could feel tears in her eyes.

There had to be something she could do! Something to make the cookie stick together?

Suddenly, she had an idea. She knew if you sucked on raisins, they got mushy and sticky. Maybe that would make good cookie glue?

She picked up one raisin. She put it in

her mouth. It tasted pretty good. She put in another one.

She chewed them up just a little.

They tasted so good, she wanted to swallow them. But she didn't.

Instead, she spit them out in her hand.

"Oooh, gross!" Tiffany said. She was standing up by Katie's desk, looking down at her.

Katie stuck out her tongue.

"Eeew!" Tiffany said. She made a blucky face and turned away.

Katie didn't care.

She took the chewed-up raisins and pressed them onto the cookie between the top and bottom part. She put one on either side of the nose.

Good! They stuck.

She leaned back and looked at it.

It was stuck together, the top and bottom were. Sort of. But it looked weird now, like it had three noses.

And the mouth was still broken in two.

Next to her, Katie could hear Amelia and Irma, still whispering.

Katie picked up some other raisins and began sucking them.

She got them good and chewy. She looked to see if Tiffany was looking. She wasn't.

Katie spit the raisins out into her hand.

She pasted them to the mouth.

But she must have pressed too hard. Because the mouth crumpled under her fingers.

"Stinky!" she whispered to herself. And then she said the baddest words she could think of. "Stupid, stupid, stinky, rat and a snake and a bug."

"Has everyone put their Secret Santa present on my desk?" Mrs. Henry said then.

Katie took a quick look around.

Everyone was nodding.

Katie slid the cookie into the little Christmas bag, and then into her desk.

She nodded, too. Just a little lie this time.

She'd have to figure out how to fix this. She couldn't give Obie a rotten, smushed-up cookie.

So for the whole rest of that day, that's all she could think of: Obie. And what to give him.

She worried all the way through lunch-time. She worried when they were on the playground for afternoon recess.

And she didn't even have a best friend to play with on the playground, either.

Instead, she played with Obie and Bobby and Arthur. She didn't like being Power Rangers, but it was better than being lonely.

They played hard, chasing each other. And then Arthur fell down. Hard. His knee got all bloody.

Mrs. Henry sent him inside to the nurse.

Katie wished she'd gotten hurt. Sometimes, Mrs. Holt, the nurse, let them have lollipops.

And that's when Katie got an idea.

Lollipops! Nurse lollipops. Obie loved lollipops.

Katie smiled.

She couldn't wait for recess to be over.

Off to the
Nurse's Office

As soon as they were back in the class-room, Katie raised her hand.

"Yes, Katie?" Mrs. Henry said.

"I have a headache," Katie said. She made her face look very sad.

Mrs. Henry frowned. "Put your head down on your desk for a while," she said. "You look hot. I think you were running too hard with the boys out there."

Katie shook her head. "I think I need a Band-Aid," she said.

"For a headache?" Mrs. Henry said.

Katie heard Amelia making that hissy snake laugh again.

Katie felt her ears get hot.

"I meant an aspirin," she said.

Mrs. Henry sighed. "All right," she said. "If you must. Go to the nurse. See what she says."

Katie got up. She walked to the front of the room. She picked up the hall pass. She walked very slowly, holding her head. She even limped a little.

Out in the hall, she began to run. She ran all the way to the nurse's office.

Next to Mrs. Henry, Mrs. Holt, the nurse, was the nicest person in the whole school. She always let you get a drink of water. She gave out Band-Aids. And she gave out lollipops. But Mrs. Holt only gave out lollipops if you got really hurt.

Katie wondered if a headache counted as really hurt.

When she got to the nurse's office, she slowed down. She put a hand on her head. She limped a little more.

But no one was around to see her. Instead, there was a sign on the nurse's door. "BACK IN A MINUTE," the sign said. "PLEASE SIT AND WAIT."

There was a bench outside the door for waiting.

Katie sat down. She put her head back against the wall.

She waited a long time.

Nobody came. She got very bored. And worried. She needed those lollipops.

She stood up.

She looked all around.

Still nobody.

She looked down the hall to the principal's office. Mr. Johnson, the school custodian, was sweeping the floor outside the office door.

She waved to him.

He waved back.

Mr. Johnson was pretty nice. He smelled of licorice. Sometimes he even gave Katie some licorice strings, red ones.

Katie went back to her bench.

She waited some more. She kicked her heels against the bench. "Boring, boring, boring," she said to herself.

She looked up at the hall clock.

Half past two.

Soon it would be time for Mrs. Henry to hand out the Secret Santa presents. Then it would be time to go home. And Obie would go home without a present!

Katie stood up. She went over to the nurse's door.

Maybe Mrs. Holt was inside resting? She had nice beds in there. Katie could wake her up, maybe.

She turned the knob.

The door opened.

Katie peeked inside.

No Mrs. Holt. No nobody. Nobody in any of the beds. Nobody at the desk.

She took a big breath and looked behind her.

Still nobody.

She turned back. She looked over at Mrs. Holt's desk.

There was a glass jar on the desk. There were lollipops in the jar.

Katie looked around once more. Over her shoulder. In front of her. All around the room. She even squatted down and looked under the beds.

Nobody.

She closed the door behind her. She tiptoed over to the desk and took the top off the candy jar.

She took another big fat breath. Then she reached in and took out a lollipop.

It wasn't stealing. Mrs. Holt would give her a lollipop anyway. Probably.

Then she took two more lollipops.

She put the top back on the jar and slid the lollipops into her pocket.

She squinted up her eyes and studied the jar. Could anyone tell some lollipops were missing?

No. The jar still looked pretty full. No one could tell. No one at all.

It wasn't stealing. Not really. Not if

Mrs. Holt was going to give her a lollipop anyway.

Except that Mrs. Holt only gave one lollipop each time.

Katie chewed on her lip. Well, what if she didn't take any lollipops the next two times she got hurt? That would make up for these, wouldn't it?

She nodded.

It would make up. And Obie would have a nice present.

She tiptoed back to the door. She put her hand on the knob.

Nobody would know.

Not even Santa Claus.

Telling a Lie

Except Mr. Johnson found out something. He was sweeping under the hall bench when Katie came tiptoeing out into the hall.

"Katie!" he said.

"Oh!" Katie said.

She felt her heart going fast. Her face felt hot. The lollipops in her pocket felt hot, too.

Mr. Johnson leaned his broom against the wall. "What were you doing in there?" he said. He frowned at her, hard.

Katie shook her head. She backed

away from him. She took teensy-weensy backwards steps down the hall toward her room.

"Nothing," she said. "I wasn't doing anything."

"You're not supposed to be in there alone," Mr. Johnson said. "That sign says wait. It means wait."

"I know," Katie said. "I waited. But I had a headache."

"A headache?" Mr. Johnson said.

"Uh-huh," Katie said. "And I was looking for Mrs. Holt. But I'm going back to class now."

"Just a minute, Missy," Mr. Johnson said. He moved to stand in front of her. He looked very big.

"Did you touch anything in there?" he said.

"No!" Katie said. She could feel her face getting even hotter.

Mr. Johnson was frowning at her, a very serious look.

"Promise?" he said. "You didn't touch anything? Not a thing?"

"Nothing," Katie said. She made a little *X* on her chest. Another lie. A big one.

What if Mr. Johnson could see the lollipops in her pocket?

"No medicines?" Mr. Johnson said. "No aspirin?"

Katie looked up at him. She made a mad face. "I don't take medicine without a grown-up!" she said.

And that was the truth.

But she did take lollipops.

"I have to go back to class now," she said.

"I'm coming with you," Mr. Johnson said.

"Never mind," Katie said. "You don't have to."

"I have to," Mr. Johnson said. He walked beside her down the hall. He was so close Katie could smell the licorice smell. He kept looking down at her like he was going to say something. But he didn't. He didn't offer her any licorice, either.

When they got to the room, Katie hurried in and slid into her seat.

Mr. Johnson stayed at the door. He motioned to Mrs. Henry. She went to the door to talk to him.

Katie didn't care. She didn't even care if she was in trouble. She had a minute to do what she needed to do. She ducked her head inside her desk. She dumped the smushed cookie out of the little Christmas bag.

She slid the lollipops into it.

Her desk was littered with crumbs now.

Mice. Mrs. Henry always said that food in your desk attracted mice.

Katie didn't care. The lollipops were in the bag, and in a minute, she'd put them on Mrs. Henry's desk with the other Secret Santa presents.

She dusted cookie crumbs off her

hands. She sat up straight and tall. She took a deep breath.

Obie was going to have a good present now.

Even if she did do something bad to get it for him.

No Bad Kids

Katie had to sit in the time-out chair for the next whole day for going in the nurse's office. Mrs. Henry wasn't too mad at her, though, especially when Mrs. Holt said all her medicines were locked up anyway.

As if Katie would take medicine without permission!

But then, after Katie's day in time-out was over, the rest of the week got better.

Katie's first present from her Secret Santa was wonderful. It was a necklace made out of macaroni, and painted all different colors.

Katie put it on right away. She wore it the whole rest of the week. Amelia kept staring at it and giggling, but Katie didn't care. She thought it was beautiful.

Another of Katie's presents was a huge chocolate chip cookie, her favorite kind, and on the third day, a Christmas tree cookie.

They weren't smashed or broken or anything.

Katie wondered how her Secret Santa person had managed that.

On Thursday, Katie's present was a drawing of two girls holding hands. It said, "Best Friends."

It made Katie a little sad, because she didn't have a best friend. But it was a nice drawing, anyway. It was covered with sparkles and stickers — bear stickers, Katie's favorite. Katie put it carefully between the pages of her reader so it wouldn't get wrinkled and so she could look at it a lot.

Things were good with Obie, too, because he was loving his Secret Santa presents. He liked his lollipops, and he loved his two airplane drawings. Daddy had helped Katie make them one night when Obie was at the store with Mom. And he really loved the book she had made for him. She had done a bunch of drawings with stickers and stuff, and taped the pages together to be a little book.

By Thursday night, Katie was feeling much happier. There was just one more day of school, and on that day, they'd find out who was their Secret Santa. And then it would be Christmas Eve and church stuff. And then it would be Christmas Day. Katie was so excited she could hardly wait. Even though she still had her worries. She lay on her bed before supper that night, thinking.

The first worry was that even though she kept trying to be good, she just kept being bad. She wondered how grown-ups were able to stay good and not get in trouble.

The other worry was that she still had no best friend. Amelia was still being a meanie. So Katie hadn't even given Amelia back her favorite barrette yet.

Katie made a big sigh and hugged her bear.

When Mom called her to supper, she went downstairs, still carrying Big Bear.

She helped Mom put Baby-Child in his high chair. He was saying his favorite word over and over again. It was "Gruh!" He used it for everything. It meant *up*, and *down*, and *yes*, and *no*, and *play*, and *eat*.

Katie thought that now it meant play. So she gave him a spoon to bang on the high-chair tray.

When everybody sat down, Katie put Big Bear in the chair next to her.

Daddy looked around the table. "We all remember about helping at church on Christmas Eve, right?" Daddy said. "We're going to bring toys and food for homeless families, remember?"

"I remember," Sam said. He didn't sound happy.

"I remember," Matt said. He didn't sound happy, either.

"I don't mind," Obie said. "I like giving presents."

"Me too," Katie said.

She looked across the table and smiled at Daddy.

Daddy gave her a little secret smile back. Katie thought she knew what he was thinking, what they were both thinking — about Obie's Secret Santa presents.

Baby-Child began waving his spoon. "Gruh, gruh, gruh!" he yelled.

Katie thought it meant he was hungry.

Mom must have thought so, too.

She held out a spoon of mushy orange stuff to him.

Baby-Child opened his mouth. He ate the orange stuff. He smushed it around. He spit it back out. Orange stuff dribbled down his chin.

"Yuck!" Katie said.

"You used to look like that," Matthew said.

"Worse, even," Sam said. "You mashed food into your hair."

"So," Katie said. "You did, too, I bet."

"Didn't," Sam said. "Did I, Mom?"

Mom smiled. "All babies are messy," she said.

"Katie was the messiest, though," Sam said. "Right, Mom?"

"You're such a brat!" Katie said.

"Children!" Mom said, with that warning sound.

"Why do I have to have brothers, anyway!" Katie said.

"You like me, right?" Obie said.

Katie just made a face. Of course she liked him. He was her twin.

She just didn't like her big brothers. Sometimes. Or even Baby-Child. Sometimes.

"Why do we have to have a sister?" Sam said.

"Children!" Mom said again.

Everybody was quiet for a minute. Mom spooned some more orange stuff into

Baby-Child. It stayed in. But his cheeks bulged out. Katie could tell he was going to spit it back out soon.

"Will there be babies at the church thing, Daddy?" Obie said.

"Probably," Daddy said.

"Homeless babies?" Katie said. She made her eyes get wide.

"I'm afraid so," Daddy said.

"With no toys and no food?" Katie said.

"They'll have them if we bring them," Mom said. She was smiling.

Katie made a frowny face. "What about Santa?" she said. "He'll bring food and toys to them. Right?"

Daddy looked down at his plate. He seemed to be thinking.

Everybody was quiet.

Even dumb old Sam and Matt got quiet.

Katie looked across the table to Obie. He had that frown he got when he was worried or sad. She thought she knew why. He was thinking about Tiffany, what Tiffany had said. That bad thing about Santa Claus.

Mom said, "Santa does come to them. It's just that he . . ."

"Needs help," Matthew said. "He needs us to help."

"How come?" Katie said.

"Well," Daddy said slowly. "Didn't your teacher say this was a season of magic?"

Katie nodded.

"I think she's right," Daddy said. "At this season, we all try to do good. Santa does good. We do good. That's the magic, I think. That's real Santa magic."

"Really?" Katie said. "Doing good stuff?"

Daddy nodded.

"Then there is a Santa?" Katie said. "Tiffany said there wasn't."

Daddy shook his head. "I guess she just doesn't know about Santa magic," he said.

Katie looked across the table at Obie.

He was smiling down at his plate.

Mom and Daddy were smiling at Sam and Matt.

Baby-Child was trying to feed himself, shoving orange stuff all over his face.

Katie sighed. She picked at the table-cloth. "But what about the bad kids, the ones who don't do good?" she said quietly. She pulled a thread loose from the cloth and wound it around her finger. "He doesn't come to bad kids, right?"

Daddy smiled. "Of course he does," he said. "He comes to everyone. But you don't have to worry." He looked all around the table. "There are no bad kids here."

Katie just sighed again.

Daddy reached over and took her hand.

"Not a single bad kid here," he said. "And that's the truth."

Good Stuff

As soon as dinner was over, Katie went right to her room. She kept thinking about Santa magic. About doing good stuff. She had something important to do.

She took Amelia's barrette out of her jacket pocket.

It was all covered with dirt and mud. There were tiny pebbles stuck in the middle of the flower. The diamonds didn't sparkle at all.

Katie took it to the bathroom.

She filled the sink with water. She put

in soap. She dropped in the barrette.

Then she took the nail brush. She rubbed and scrubbed at the barrette until it was all shiny again.

She held it up and looked at it. All the pebbles and mud were gone. It looked like new. Shiny and sparkly and everything.

Katie took it to her room. She wrapped it in some soft tissues. She put it in her backpack.

She couldn't wait for the next day and school.

In the morning, she and Obie raced to the bus stop. Katie was singing "Rudolph," and Obie joined in, too. He seemed to forget that he didn't like that song.

Katie hadn't felt so happy in a long time. Daddy had come to her room the night before, and told her to make a list. He said not to put down the bad things. To forget them. But list all the good things she'd done.

Together they had made a big, long list. Katie had it in her backpack now. Daddy said she should keep looking at it, to see what a good kid she really was.

The first thing on the list was Obie. She'd invited Obie to share her special weekend with her grandmas.

She'd made great Secret Santa presents for Obie.

Also, she helped a lot with Baby-Child.

She'd been very good their day in the city.

She didn't fight with her big brothers so much anymore.

At school, she had found the lost rabbit. (Even though she didn't tell Daddy it was her fault he'd gotten lost.)

She got to school on time and did her homework every single day. Katie hadn't even thought of that as being especially good. Daddy reminded her.

And the best thing of all, Daddy said, was that she was loving. And good. A really good kid.

Katie added, in her head, a few other good things about herself, things she didn't want to tell Daddy:

She hadn't snuck out in the night.

She hadn't kicked Amelia, even though she had felt like it.

Now Katie smiled to herself.

"Guess what, Obie," she said, as they sat on the curb waiting for the bus. "I did some magic last night. Santa magic."

"What?" Obie said.

"I cleaned up Amelia's barrette. I'm going to give it back to her," Katie said.

"I thought you already did," Obie said.

Katie shook her head. "I was mad at her."

"Oh," Obie said.

"And know what else?" Katie said.

"What?" Obie said.

Katie made her voice very quiet. She looked around to see if anyone else could hear. There was no one around. "I'm going to tell Mrs. Henry about losing Ken," she said. "I'm going to tell her it was my fault."

"It was?" Obie said.

Katie nodded.

"Not on purpose, though," Obie said.

"Still," Katie said.

"I did some Santa magic, too," Obie said.

"You did?" Katie said. "What?"

Obie dug one foot deep into the snow by the curb. "I made an airplane drawing for Santa. I'm going to leave it for him Christmas Eve."

"He'll like that," Katie said.

And then the other kids got there and the bus got there, and they all went to school. Everybody was very excited, because it was the last day.

And everybody was very excited because they got to tell about Secret Santa.

Some of the kids had already guessed theirs.

Katie didn't know who hers was, though.

She didn't think Obie knew his, either.

The only bad thing was that Amelia still didn't sit with her on the bus. And Amelia kept looking at her and laughing.

And I don't care! Katie thought.

There was just one final thing to do. Katie felt in the pocket of her jacket. There was sixty-three cents in an envelope there, all the money she had in her piggy bank.

As soon as they got in school, Katie took a little detour. She went down the hall to the nurse's office.

The door was still closed.

Katie looked all around.

No one. Not even Mr. Johnson.

She bent over. She slid her envelope under the door. She straightened up and started back for her room.

She had paid for the lollipops. And she hadn't had to tell.

She raced back down the hall to her room.

Then, right away, she went up to the front to talk to Mrs. Henry. She told Mrs.

Henry everything. She told about Ken. She even told about peeking at the word *Hanukkah*.

Mrs. Henry must have had Santa magic, too. Because she didn't even get mad.

And she hugged Katie for a long time.

Best Friends

At the end of the day, Mrs. Henry had everyone sit up straight and tall.

Then she went up and down the aisles, giving out each person's Secret Santa present. This time, the present had the giver's name on it.

Nobody could look till everybody had theirs.

Katie kept looking over at Obie. She knew he'd be so excited when he saw her name. And she knew he'd love his present. She had saved the best for last. It was a box where he could keep his airplane drawings.

Mom had helped her make it out of a cookie box. Katie had glued seashells all over it. She had collected the shells last summer.

He would love it.

Katie sat up straight and tall and waited for Mrs. Henry to bring her her present.

Mrs. Henry patted Katie when she put the present down in front of her.

It was a flat present.

It looked like a drawing or a card.

Katie wondered if it was another best friends card.

She snuck a look at Tiffany.

Could mean old Tiffany want to be best friends?

But Tiffany wasn't looking back. She was looking over at Irma.

Katie looked at Amelia then.

Amelia was looking back. But when she saw Katie looking, she looked away.

Katie looked away, too. She thought about Santa. She sighed. Even Santa couldn't give you a best friend.

Mrs. Henry said, "All right, boys and girls. You may open your presents now. And then you may get up and go thank your Secret Santa."

Everybody began opening presents.

Katie could hear people going "Ooh" and "Oh." Some people were laughing.

Katie tore the paper off her present.

It was another drawing like the first, only better. It had two girls. They were holding hands. The words over their heads said, "Best Friends." Their clothes were all sparkly with glitter. One girl's dress was pink, Katie's favorite color. The other girl's dress was red, Amelia's favorite color. There were names on the dresses.

The pink dress said "Katie."

The red dress said "Amelia."

The card told Katie's Secret Santa's name. It said: "Amelia."

Katie looked at Amelia.

"You?" Katie said. "You're my Secret Santa?"

Amelia nodded. She frowned. She looked a little mad.

"Oh," Katie said.

"That's why I couldn't tell," Amelia said. She sounded mad, too.

"Oh," Katie said again. Then she added, "You have to look at yours."

"I already did," Amelia said. "It's from Arthur. It's a cookie."

"I meant this one," Katie said.

She reached in her desk. She took out the barrette, all wrapped in tissues.

She put the tissue package on Amelia's desk.

Amelia made another frowny face. But she unrolled the tissues.

She looked up at Katie. "My favorite barrette!" she said. "I lost it!"

"I know," Katie said. "I found it."

"It's shiny," Amelia said.

"I shined it," Katie said.

Amelia smiled.

Katie smiled back. She touched her

macaroni necklace. "I like this a lot," she said. "The other stuff you gave me, too."

Amelia nodded. "I know," she said.

Katie turned away. "Want to sit with me on the bus?" she said.

She didn't look at Amelia when she said it.

Instead, she looked over at Irma.

Irma was talking to Tiffany. They were laughing together. It looked like Tiffany was Irma's Secret Santa.

It looked like maybe Tiffany didn't hate Irma anymore.

"Okay," Amelia said.

"Good," Katie said.

"Because we're best friends, right?" Amelia said.

"Right," Katie said.

She smiled at Amelia.

Amelia smiled back.

Katie thought of what Mrs. Henry had said about a magic season. She thought about what Daddy had said about Santa magic.

She thought about having a best friend again.

She thought Santa was wonderful.

And she still hoped that he could bring a trampoline. And a castle tea party set.

To a mostly good kid.

LITTLE 🍎 APPLE®

There are fun times ahead with kids just like you in Little Apple books! Once you take a bite out of a Little Apple—you'll want to read more!

Reading Excitement for Kids with BIG Appetites!

☐ NA42833-0 **Catwings** Ursula K. LeGuin **$2.95**

☐ NA42832-2 **Catwings Return** Ursula K. LeGuin **$2.95**

☐ NA41821-1 **Class Clown** Johanna Hurwitz **$2.75**

☐ NA43868-9 **The Haunting of Grade Three**
Grace Maccarone **$2.75**

☐ NA40966-2 **Rent A Third Grader** B.B. Hiller **$2.99**

☐ NA41944-7 **The Return of the Third Grade Ghost Hunters**
Grace Maccarone **$2.75**

☐ NA44477-8 **Santa Claus Doesn't Mop Floors**
Debra Dadey and Marcia Thornton Jones **$2.99**

☐ NA42031-3 **Teacher's Pet** Johanna Hurwitz **$2.99**

☐ NA43411-X **Vampires Don't Wear Polka Dots**
Debra Dadey and Marcia Thornton Jones **$2.99**

☐ NA44061-6 **Werewolves Don't Go to Summer Camp**
Debra Dadey and Marcia Thornton Jones **$2.99**

Available wherever you buy books...or use the coupon below.

SCHOLASTIC INC., Box 7502, 2931 East McCarty Street, Jefferson City, MO 65102

Please send me the books I have checked above. I am enclosing $ _____ (please add $2.00 to cover shipping and handling). Send check or money order—no cash or C.O.D.s please.

Name _____

Address _____

City _____ State/Zip _____

Please allow four to six weeks for delivery. Offer good in the U.S.A. only. Sorry, mail orders are not available to residents of Canada. Prices subject to change.

LA595